WILD FLOWERS OF KASHMIR

WILD FLOWERS OF KASHMIR

B. O. COVENTRY

GYAN

Published by

GYAN

Gyan Publishing House
5, Ansari Road
Daryaganj, New Delhi-110002
Phone: 011-47034999, 9811692060
E-mail: books@gyanbooks.com

Distribution Network
gyanbooks.com
India, USA, Canada, UK, Australia

ISBN: 978-93-7447-608-6 (PB)

First Published, 1927

2nd Impression 2026

Printed at: Gyan Press, Delhi.

WILD FLOWERS OF KASHMIR
Author: B. O. COVENTRY

PRIMULA NIVALIS, *Pall.*, Var. MACROPHYLLA, *Pax.*, NEAR SONSA NAG IN THE LIDDAR VALLEY AT 13,000'.

WILD FLOWERS OF KASHMIR

(SERIES II)

BY

B. O. COVENTRY, F.C.H.,

CONSERVATOR OF FORESTS

WITH DESCRIPTIONS AND
COLOURED ILLUSTRATIONS OF FIFTY SPECIES
REPRODUCED FROM
DIRECT COLOUR PHOTOGRAPHS

LONDON:

RAITHBY, LAWRENCE & CO., LTD.

1927

CONTENTS.

INTRODUCTION.

EXPLANATION OF THE BOTANICAL TERMS USED.

Achene, a small, dry, one-seeded fruit.

Acuminate, when the apex of a leaf is suddenly narrowed and then prolonged to a long point.

Acute, when the apex of a leaf is sharp-pointed, forming a narrow angle.

Adnate, when dissimilar parts are united.

Alternate, when the leaves are arranged singly at the nodes, and not in pairs or whorls of several leaves at the same node.

Amplexicaul, when the base of a sessile leaf clasps the stem.

Annual, lasting for only one year.

Apiculate, when the apex of a leaf is suddenly narrowed and terminated with a short-pointed tip.

Ascending, when the stem grows obliquely upwards.

Auricle, a small appendage resembling the lobe of an ear.

Axil, the upper angle between the base of a leaf and the stem.

Axillary, when growing from the axil of a leaf.

Bi-fid, when a leaf is cut into two narrow segments, the cut not extending much beyond the middle.

Bi-pinnate, when the leaf is twice pinnately divided.

Bi-sexual, when a flower has both stamens and carpels.

Bract, a small scale-like or leaf-like organ immediately beneath a flower or cluster of flowers, or on the peduncle or pedicel.

Bracteole, a small secondary bract.

Caducous, falling off early.

Campanulate, bell-shaped.

Capitate, with a rounded head.

Capsule, a dry fruit which splits open whilst on the plant to set the seeds free, and formed from several united carpels.

Cauline, when inserted on the stem.

Ciliate, when the margin of a leaf is fringed with hairs.

Clawed, when the lower part of the petal is narrowed to a slender stalk.

Compound, when a leaf is divided to the petiole or midrib into several distinct leaflets.

Connate, when the bases of two opposite leaves are united.

Connivent, when the tips of two organs converge together.

Cordate, when the base of a leaf is produced downwards, forming a rounded lobe on each side of the petiole, *e.g.* heart-shaped.

Corymb, an inflorescence in which the pedicels start from different points, the lower ones being longer than the upper ones, so that all the flowers are brought to the same level.

Crenate, with blunt, rounded teeth.

Cuneate, wedge-shaped.

Cyme, an inflorescence in which the main axis and lateral axes are each terminated by a flower, and the flowering proceeds outwards and downwards.

Deciduous, when the parts of a flower fall immediately after fertilisation of the ovary.

Decompound, when a leaf is several times compound.

Dehisce, to split open.

Denticulate, when the margin of a leaf is cut into small triangular teeth directed outwards, not forwards or backwards.

Dichotomous, when a stem is repeatedly branched in such a manner that the branches are always forked or in pairs.

Didynamous, when there are four stamens, two long ones and two short ones.

Digitate, when the leaflets of a compound leaf all spring from the top of the petiole like the fingers of a hand.

Dilated, expanded equally on all sides.

Disc, (1) a protuberance from the receptacle of the flower which is usually annular and cushion-like between the calyx and carpels ; (2) the central portion of a flower-head as distinguished from the border or ray.

Divaricate, spreading widely apart.

Emarginate, when the apex of a leaf has a decided terminal notch.

Entire, when the margin of a leaf is not cut in any way.

Exstipulate, without stipules.

Fascicle, a bundle.

Filiform, very slender, thread-like.

Fimbriate, with a fringe of hairs.

Follicle, a fruit formed from a single carpel, which when ripe splits open down one side only.

Free central placentation, when the ovules are attached to a central column rising from the base of the ovary, and unattached to the sides.

Gamopetalous, when the petals are united.

Gibbous, a pouch-like swelling on one side.

Glabrous, smooth, without any hairs.

Glabrescent, almost glabrous, with few hairs.

Glandular hairy, when the hairs have a swelling at the tip from which some oily or sticky substance exudes.

Glaucous, with a bluish-grey or bluish-green tinge.

Hastate, like a spear head.

Herbaceous, with the soft texture and green colour of the stem leaves.

Hermaphrodite, when a flower possesses both stamens and pistil.

Hirsute, with long and rather stiff hairs.

Hispid, with long, stiff, bristle-like hairs.

Imbricate, when close together and overlapping, like the tiles or shingles on a roof.

Inferior, when the ovary is adnate to the calyx with the petals and stamens inserted above it.

Involucre, the collective name for the bracts when they are whorled below a flower-head, umbel or other cluster of flowers, *e.g.* the bracts enclosing the flower-heads in the Natural Order Compositæ.

Lanceolate, when a leaf is about three times or more as long as broad, broadest below the middle and the summit tapering to a point, *e.g.* like a lance head.

Ligule, the extended strap-like part of the corolla of the ray flowers in some species of the N. O. Compositæ.

Limb, the upper part of a petal when it is narrowed below into a stalk, or the upper expanded part of a gamopetalous corolla when the lower portion is narrowed to a tube.

Linear, when the leaf is long and narrow, and of more or less equal width throughout its length.

Lineolate, marked with fine lines.

Mucronate, when the apex of a leaf abruptly terminates in a short, sharp point.

Nectary, a part of the flower which secretes sweet honey juices.

Nodes, the points on a stem at which the leaves are inserted.

Ob-lanceolate, when a leaf is about three times or more longer than broad, broadest above the middle, and tapering downwards to a point, *e.g.* the reverse of lanceolate.

Ob-ovate, when a leaf is scarcely twice as long as broad, and broader above the middle.

Obtuse, when the apex of a leaf is blunt, rounded, or wide-angled.

Odd-pinnate, when a leaf is pinnate, with an odd terminal leaflet.

Opposite, when two leaves grow from the same node on opposite sides of the stem.

Orbicular, when a leaf is of a circular shape.

Ovate, when a leaf is scarcely twice as long as broad, and broader below the middle.

Panicle, when the rachis divides into branches bearing more than one flower.

Pappus, the name of a calyx consisting of hairs as in the Natural Order Compositæ.

Partite, divided almost to the base.

Pedicel, the stalk of a single flower, when the peduncle bears several flowers.

Peduncle, the stalk of a flower, or cluster of flowers.

Peltate, when the petiole of a leaf is attached to the lower surface of the blade of the leaf, usually near the centre.

Perianth, the collective name for both the sepals and petals. The term is usually used when there is little distinction between the sepals and petals, or when one of these whorls is absent.

Persistent, when any part of the flower does not fall early, but remains until the fruit is mature.

Petaloid, when the sepals have the appearance of petals.

Pinnate, when the leaflets of a compound leaf are arranged on each side of the rachis like the branches of a feather.

Pinnatifid, when a leaf is cut on the margin into lobes arranged like the leaflets of a pinnate leaf, the incisions not extending beyond the middle.

Pinnatipartite, similar to pinnatifid, but with deeper incisions extending almost to the rachis.

Pinnatisect, similar to pinnatifid, but with deeper incisions extending to the rachis.

Prostrate, when a stem grows horizontally, lying on the ground.

Pubescent, with soft, short hairs.

Rachis, the prolongation of the petiole, or peduncle, on which the leaflets or flowers are inserted.

Raceme, when the flowers are borne on pedicels along an undivided rachis.

Radical, when the leaves grow directly from the rootstock.

Receptacle, the top of the peduncle inside the calyx on which the parts of the flower are inserted.

Reflexed, bent abruptly backwards or downwards.

Reticulate, when the veins in a leaf are arranged like a net.

Rootstock, that part of the plant which forms the junction between root and stem, or root and leaves in the case of leaves growing direct from the rootstock. It may either be erect above ground, or prostrate, growing horizontally above or below ground, producing buds on the upper surface from which stems or leaves develop, and roots on the lower surface.

Rotate, when the limb of a gamopetalous corolla is flat, with a very short tube, resembling a wheel.

Saccate, swollen, forming a pouch or little bag.

Saggitate, when the base of a leaf is produced downwards into two pointed lobes, like an arrow head.

Salver-shaped, similar to rotate, but with a long corolla-tube.

Scabrid, when the surface of a leaf is rough to the touch, owing to small, hard, scattered tubercles, or short, stiff hairs.

Scape, the name for a leafless flower stalk growing direct from the rootstock.

Scarious, when the texture is thin and dry as opposed to green and succulent.

Scorpioid, when the rachis of a raceme or spike is coiled from the tip.

Serrate, when the margin of a leaf is cut into sharp teeth, like the teeth of a saw.

Sessile, without a stalk or petiole.

Setaceous, bristle-like.

Sheath, the expanded base of a petiole.

Simple, when a leaf is undivided into separate leaflets.

Spathulate, when a leaf is broad and rounded at the apex and narrow at the base, like a spatula.

Spike, when the flowers are sessile along a simple undivided rachis, *i.e.* similar to a raceme, but with sessile flowers.

Stellate, star-like.

Stipules, small scale-like or leaf-like organs at the base of a leaf.

Subulate, when shaped like a shoemaker's awl.

Sub-sessile, almost sessile.

Superior, when the ovary is free from the calyx, with the petals and stamens inserted below it.

Ternate, when a compound leaf is divided into three separate leaflets springing from the same point.

Tesselated, marked with small square or oblong patches like a mosaic.

Tomentose, densely covered with short, soft matted hairs.

Torulose, with constrictions at intervals.

Truncate, when the apex of a leaf is abruptly cut off.

Tuberous, swollen into a rounded form.

Turbinate, with the shape of a top, or inverted cone.

Umbel, when several pedicels radiate from the top of a peduncle, and are all of about the same length.

Urceolate, when the calyx or corolla is tubular with a constriction below the mouth, *e.g.* urn-shaped.

Valvate, when the margins of sepals or petals meet together without overlapping.

Ventricose, swollen on one side.

Whorl, when several leaves or other organs are arranged in a circle round a central axis.

CLASSIFICATION.

The following key shows how the Natural Orders represented in this volume are classified into classes, sub-classes and series.

Class I. **Dicotyledons.** Plants with the parts of the flower in fours or fives or multiples of these; leaves with the veins branching in a network manner: two cotyledons (rudimentary leaves) to the embryo in the seed.

Sub-class 1. **Polypetalæ.** Petals not united.

Series (i). **Thalamifloræ.** Parts of the flower inserted on the receptacle. Petals and stamens inserted below the ovary : ovary free from the calyx.

Natural Orders:
1. Ranunculaceæ.
2. Nymphæaceæ.
3. Papaveraceæ.
4. Fumariaceæ.
5. Cruciferæ.

Series (ii). **Discifloræ.** The receptacle usually expanded into a disc between the petals and ovary.

Series (iii). **Calycifloræ.** Parts of the flower (petals and stamens) inserted on the calyx, the stamens being inserted above the base of the ovary.

Natural Orders:
6. Leguminoseæ.
7. Rosaceæ.
8. Saxifragaceæ.
9. Hamamelideæ.
10. Onagraceæ.

Sub-class 2. **Gamopetalæ.** Petals united.

Series (i). With the ovary inferior.

Natural Orders:
11. Caprifoliaceæ.
12. Compositæ.
13. Campanulaceæ.

Series (ii). With the ovary superior.

Natural Orders:
14. Ericaceæ.
15. Primulaceæ.
16. Gentianaceæ.
17. Boragineæ.
18. Solanaceæ.
19. Scrophularineæ.

Sub-class 3. **Monochlamydeæ.** Plants with no perianth, or with either the calyx or corolla absent.

Series (i). With the ovary inferior.

Series (ii). With the ovary superior.

Natural Order ... 20. Polygonaceæ.

Class II. **Monocotyledons.** Plants with the parts of the flower in threes or multiples of three ; veins of the leaves more or less parallel ; one cotyledon to the embryo in the seed.

Sub-class 4. **Petaloideæ.** The perianth with at least one whorl like petals.

Series (i). With the ovary inferior.

Series (ii). With the ovary superior.

Natural Order ... 21. Liliaceæ.

An index showing the species illustrated in this book, classified into their Natural Orders, is given at the end of the book.

CLEMATIS MONTANA, *Ham.* (Pl. I.)

Large Himalayan Clematis.

Nat. Order. *Ranunculaceæ.* The Buttercup Family.

Name. The generic name is derived from the Greek word "*klema*," a vine-twig, referring to the twining character of the leaf-stalks. The specific name is from the Latin word "*montanus*," referring to the mountainous habitat of the plant.

Description. A tall, robust perennial climber, producing a great profusion of large handsome white flowers which over-lie shrubs and low trees like a mantle of snow.

Stem, tough and woody, much branched, climbing to 20′ or more.

Leaves, exstipulate, fascicled, long petioled, divided into 3 distinct leaflets, petioles twining round their support. **Leaflets** 3, ovate, toothed or incised, acute.

Flowers, white, 2–4″ in diam., on long peduncles arranged in fascicles, each peduncle bearing a solitary flower.

Sepals, 4, petaloid, white, widely spreading valvate in bud.

Petals, 0.

Stamens, many, glabrous.

Carpels, many, free, each with a single ovule.

Fruit, a cluster of free achenes, each terminated with a long feathery style.

Distinguishing characters. The large white solitary flowers in fascicles easily distinguishes it from other species.

Flowering Season. April, May.

CLEMATIS MONTANA—*continued.*

Locality. Abundant throughout the Valley, at elevations of 4–10,000′; plentiful along the Jhelum-valley road in the spring.

Distribution. Temperate Himalaya from the Indus to the Bramaputra, ascending to 12,000′; Sikkim, Khasia Hills.

CLEMATIS MONTANA, *Ham.*

CLEMATIS GRAVEOLENS, *Lindl.* (Pl. II.)

Odoriferous Clematis.

Nat. Order. *Ranunculaceæ.* The Buttercup Family.

Name. The generic name is from the Greek "*klema*," a vine-twig, referring to the twining character of the leaf-stalks. The specific name is the Latin word for "strong smelling."

Description. A tall, slender perennial climber, with pinnately compound leaves, and producing a profusion of pale lemon-yellow coloured flowers.

Stem, tough but rather slender, much branched, climbing to 10′ or more.

Leaves, exstipulate, opposite, pinnately decompound. **Leaflets**, small, ½-1″ in length, toothed or incised, or 3-lobed or 3-partite, the terminal leaflet the largest, glabrous.

Flowers, dull lemon-yellow or cream coloured, 1½-2″ diam., in panicles of few (3-7) flowers, and also solitary or long peduncles in the axils of the leaves, the peduncle often bearing a pair of small bracts.

Sepals, usually 4 or 5, spreading, broad, elliptic, obtuse, petaloid, pubescent on the outer surface and densely tomentose on the inner surface.

Petals, 0.

Stamens, many, filaments hairy.

Carpels, many, free.

Fruit, a cluster of free pubescent achenes, each terminated with a long feathery style.

Distinguishing characters. Flowers in panicles, sepals spreading, filaments hairy, distinguish it from other species except *Clematis orientalis*, to which it is very closely allied.

Clematis graveolens, *Lindl.* Panicles with few flowers, 3-7 ; sepals elliptic, acute.

Clematis orientalis, *Linn.* Panicles with many flowers, sepals ovate, acuminate, but intermediates also occur, so that these two species are almost indistinguishable one from the other.

Flowering Season. September, October.

Locality. Abundant throughout the Valley, usually at fairly low elevations of about 3–7,000′, in open sunny situations. Plentiful along the Jhelum-valley road between Ghari and Baramulla, where it is very conspicuous with its profusion of pale yellow flowers, overlying shrubs and small trees in the month of October.

Distribution. Western Temperate Himalaya from Kashmir to Kumaon, ascending to 11,000′.

CLEMATIS GRAVEOLENS, *Lindl.*

II

ANEMONE BIFLORA, *DC.* (Pl. III.)

Tuberous Anemone.

Nat. Order. *Ranunculaceæ.* The Buttercup Family.

Name. The generic name is from the Greek "*anemos*," the wind, referring to the exposed situations in which some species grow.

Description. A small tuberous perennial, with radical leaves, and a leafless scape bearing 1–3 white or carmine flowers, which become dull red or brownish when over-mature.

Rootstock, tuberous, ovoid, about ¾″ in length by ½″ in breadth.

Leaves, all radical, 1-2″ in diam., long petioled, 3-partite or 3-foliolate, the leaf segments rounded or cuneate, deeply cut into narrow lobes or toothed. When the first flower opens the young leaves are barely ½″ in diam. and frequently red-purple on the lower surface.

Flowers, appearing at the same time as the leaves; when freshly opened pure white or bright carmine or white diffused with carmine, turning brownish or dull red when over-mature; 1-1¼″ in diam. on a leafless scape bearing 1-3 pedicelled flowers with 3 involucral bracts at the base of the pedicels. When the first flower opens there is usually only one other flower bud visible and the scape only 1-1½″ in length, but on maturing the scape becomes elongated to 4-8″ in length, bearing 3 long, pedicelled flowers, the lateral pedicels with a pair of bracteoles similar to, but smaller, than the involucral bracts, the terminal pedicel being without bracteoles. **Involucral bracts,** usually 3, sessile, cut into linear lobes to about the middle, the lobes entire, incised or toothed.

Sepals, 5, petaloid, broad, elliptic, obtuse.

Petals, 0.

ANEMONE BIFLORA—*continued.*

Stamens, many, filaments often carmine.

Carpels, many, free, with short carmine styles.

Fruit, a cluster of many free achenes, densely covered with white wool (which only becomes visible when the carpels are mature).

Distinguishing characters. The tuberous rootstock and densely woolly achenes distinguish it from other species.

Flowering Season. February, March. One of the earliest flowers to appear in the neighbourhood of Srinagar.

Locality. At 4–6,000′ on open, dry, grassy or stony slopes. Very abundant at the foot of the Takht hill at Srinagar and alongside the road between Baramulla and Srinagar.

Distribution. Turkestan and eastwards to Persia.

ANEMONE BIFLORA, *DC.*

ANEMONE FALCONERI, *Thoms.* (Pl. IV.)

Falconer's Anemone.

Nat. Order. *Ranunculaceæ.* The Buttercup Family.

Name. The generic name is from the Greek "*anemos*," the wind, referring to the exposed situations in which some species grow. The specific name has been given in honour of the botanist, Falconer.

Description. A small, herbaceous plant with long petioled radical leaves and small white solitary flowers on long slender peduncles.

Rootstock, short, stout, fibrous-rooted.

Leaves, all radical, 2-3″ diam., numerous, long petioled, hairy on both surfaces, 3-partite, the segments lobed and toothed.

Flowers, white (rarely diffused with red-purple on the outside), $\frac{1}{3}$-$\frac{1}{2}$″ diam., solitary on long, slender, hairy scapes 3-6″ in length ; several scapes from the same rootstock. **Involucral bracts,** 3, oblong, usually entire, about $\frac{1}{2}$″ in length.

Sepals, 5-7, petaloid, white, narrow, elliptic, obtuse or acute.

Petals, 0.

Stamens, many.

Carpels, many, free.

Fruit, a cluster of achenes, each with a short style ; achenes oblong, angled, silky, not embedded in dense wool.

Distinguishing characters. The small, white, solitary flowers distinguish it from other species.

Flowering Season. April, May.

ANEMONE FALCONERI—*continued*.

Locality. At 5–8,000′ in shady woods. Frequent in the woods between Tangmarg and Gulmarg.

Distribution. West Temperate Himalaya : Hazara.

ANEMONE FALCONERI, *Thoms.*

IV

PARAQUILEGIA GRANDIFLORA,

Drum & Hutch. (Pl. v.)

Large-flowered Rock Anemone.

Nat. Order. *Ranunculaceæ.*

Name. In Hooker's *Flora of British India* this plant is described under *Isopyrum grandiflorum* (*Fisch*). The generic name is from the Latin "*par*," equal, and aquilegia, the generic name for the Columbines, which is derived from the Latin "*aquila*," an eagle.

Description. A beautiful little Alpine perennial rock-plant, growing in tufts, with long petioled and much divided radical leaves, and rather large white or very pale mauve solitary flowers on long slender scapes.

Rootstock, stout, bearing dense tufts of short branches clothed with long, brown bristles, the remains of previous year's leaf-stalks.

Leaves, all radical, glabrous, long petioled, 2-5″ in length, 2-3 ternately compound ; pinnules deeply cut into 1-4 narrow or broad lobes ; petioles slender, wiry, sheathing and auricled at the base.

Flowers, white or delicately tinged with pale mauve, 1-1¼″ diam., solitary on long, slender, wiry scapes ; scapes 2-6″ in length, often almost black, with 2 small bracts at some distance below the flower ; bracts about 3/16″ in length, narrow, acute, shortly petioled, the petiole dilated at the base and bearing two whitish, rounded auricles.

Sepals, 5, petaloid, white or pale mauve, oblong or elliptic, obtuse, entire, spreading.

Petals, 5, very small, about 3/16″ in length, much shorter than the sepals and stamens, bright yellow, ob-ovate-oblong, tip emarginate, recurved, margins below curved inwards and united at the base forming a small pouch.

Stamens, many.

Carpels, usually 5 (always more than 2), free; ovaries oblong with short linear styles.

Fruit, a cluster of small, free follicles, each with a short, lateral, sharp beak.

Distinguishing characters. There are four species distinguished as follows :—

Ripe carpels more or less erect, stems cæspitose, rigid.
Leaves glabrous, 2-3 ternately divided.
Seeds puberulous ... *P. grandiflora.*
Seeds glabrous ... *P. microphylla.*

Leaves minutely puberulous, usually simply trifoliolate.
P. cæspitosa.

Ripe carpels spreading, stems slender, decumbent, solitary or few.
P. uniflora.

The genus *Paraquilegia* is distinguished from *Isopyrum* by the presence of petals and more than 2 carpels.

Flowering Season. June, July.

Locality. On rocks at elevations of 11-15,000′, *e.g.*, Apharwat, Zojpal, Astan Marg.

Distribution. From Kashmir to Kumaon.

PARAQUILEGIA GRANDIFLORA, *Drum and Hutch.*

V

DELPHINIUM RANUNCULIFOLIUM,

Buttercup-leaved Larkspur. *Wall.* (Pl. VI.)

Nat. Order. *Ranunculaceæ.* The Buttercup Family.

Name. The generic name is from the Greek "*Delphis*," a dolphin, referring to the shape of the flowers. The English name for plants of this genus is " Larkspur." In Hooker's *Flora of British India* the plant is referred to under *D. elatum* (*Linn*), var. *ranunculifolium.*

Description. A tall, robust perennial with long racemes of spurred blue-purple flowers, and leaves lobed to near the middle.

Rootstock, stout, woody.

Stem, erect, stout, 2-6′ in height, often several, glabrous or hairy.

Leaves. Radical leaves, hairy, long petioled, 4-7″ in diam., orbicular or reniform, 5-7 palmately lobed to near the middle ; the lobes broadly cuneate, more or less 3-lobed and serrate. **Cauline leaves,** similar to the radical leaves, but shorter petioled, more deeply lobed, and less hairy, the upper ones often glabrous.

Flowers, dark blue-purple, 1¼-1½″ in length by 1″ in diam. in simple or branched racemes which are sometimes as much as 2′ in length. **Pedicels** 1-3″, dilated and curved at the top. **Bracts,** leafy, ovate-lanceolate, acuminate, up to 1¼″ in length, entire or the lowermost 3-lobed or toothed ; the upper flowers often with the bract about half-way up the pedicel. **Bracteoles,** 2 at the top of the pedicels, ovate-lanceolate or linear, acuminate, entire, green tinged with purple.

Sepals, 5, sub-erect, elliptic, obtuse, unequal, slightly hairy outside.

Spur, straight or slightly curved, about equal in length to the sepals, subulate (not broadly conical and inflated).

Petals, 4, small, the 2 dorsal ones spurred, oblong, black, glabrous, notched ; the 2 lateral ones clawed, black, 2-fid, densely hairy on both surfaces of the limb.

Stamens, many.

Carpels, several, free.

Fruit, a cluster of 3 free follicles.

Distinguishing characters. The subulate spur, and leaves palmately lobed to near the middle distinguishes it from other species.

Flowering Season. Middle of July to end of August.

Locality. At 10-13000′, *e.g.*, Zojpal, Shisha Nag, Bandipore Nala.

Distribution. West Temperate Himalaya, in the inner Thibetan Valleys ; Kashmir to Kumaon.

DELPHINIUM RANUNCULIFOLIUM, *Wall.*

VI

DELPHINIUM CASHMERIANUM, *Royle.*

Kashmir Larkspur. (Pl. VII.)

Nat. Order. *Ranunculaceæ.* The Buttercup Family.

Name. The generic name is from the Greek " *Delphis*," a dolphin, referring to the shape of the flowers. The English name for plants of this genus is " Larkspur."

Description. An Alpine perennial with simple, palmately lobed leaves, and large, very hairy, blue-purple flowers with a broad inflated conical spur.

Rootstock, stout and woody, crowned with the old withered remains of previous years' leaf-stalks.

Stem, erect, 6-18″ in height, but rarely above 12″ ; few leaved ; usually hairy.

Leaves. **Radical leaves,** few, 2-4½″ diam., long petioled, palmately 5-7 lobed ; the lobes cuneate-ovate, more or less 3-lobed and with few small teeth. **Cauline leaves,** the lowermost long petioled, and the uppermost short petioled, 3-5 partite with acute teeth, usually hairy on both surfaces.

Flowers, blue-purple with darker veins, 1¼-2″ in length including the spur, and about 1″ or more in diam.; in lax corymbs, the branches of the corymb bearing about 3-8 flowers on long pedicels with 2 or 3 linear bracteoles.

Sepals, 5, ¾-1¼″ in length, densely hairy, the front and lateral ones concave and inflated at the base, the dorsal one spurred.

Spur, straight or slightly curved, broadly conical and inflated, obtuse, usually rather shorter than the sepals.

Petals, black, small, 2 dorsal ones linear, long spurred, 2-fid limb ; 2 anterior ones clawed with very hairy limb.

Stamens, many.

Carpels, several, with short styles.

Fruit, a cluster of 3-7 downy follicles.

Distinguishing characters. The large, broad, inflated, hairy flowers in corymbs distinguishes it from other species, except *D. Brunonianum* (*Royle*), but this latter species has pale grey-blue very translucent flowers.

Flowering Season. August.

Locality. 11-13,000′. Abundant at Zojpal and Shisha Nag.

Distribution. West Thibet and Thibetan Himalaya, from Kashmir to Kumaon.

DELPHINIUM CASHMERIANUM, *Royle.*

EURYALE FEROX, *Salisb.* (Pl. VIII.)

Euryale.

Nat. Order. *Nymphæaceæ.* The Water-lily Family.

Name. The generic name is the name of one of Ovid's Gorgans, whose head was covered with vipers instead of hair, and refers to the fierce aspect of the plant with its sharp spines. The specific name is the Latin word for " fierce."

Description. An aquatic plant, with large round floating leaves, which are purple on the under surface, and all parts of the plant covered with long, sharp spines.

Rootstock, stout, perennial.

Leaves, 6″-1½′ in diam., oblong or orbicular, floating, with long, stout, densely prickly, flexible petioles, the upper surface wrinkled, green with red veins, covered with stout, curved prickles; the lower surface purple with very prominent white ribs bearing long, sharp spines, the ribs often as much as ½″ or more in depth near the petiole.

Flowers, 2-2½″ diam., violet or variegated white and violet, solitary at the ends of long, stout, flexible, prickly peduncles. The flowers develop under water and only emerge above the water for a short time when mature.

Sepals, 4, about 1″ in length, ovate, obtuse, thick and covered with long, sharp spines on the outer surface, valvate in bud; inner surface dark red.

Petals, numerous, oblong or elliptic, obtuse; outer ones almost equal in length to the sepals, violet; inner ones smaller, variegated white and violet or white.

Stamens, many, in bunches of 8.

Ovary, 8-celled and sunk in the thickened top of the receptacle.

EURYALE FEROX—*continued.*

Stigma, discoid, depressed, concave.

Fruit, a spongy berry covered with sharp spines, 2-4″ diam., crowned with the persistent calyx, containing about 8-20 black seeds of $\frac{1}{4}$-$\frac{1}{2}$″ diam. which ripen under water.

Distinguishing characters. No other species, readily recognised by its floating, prickly leaves which are purple on the under surface.

Flowering Season. October.

Locality. Abundant in the Dal Lake at Srinagar.

Distribution. Oudh, Eastern Bengal, China.

Uses. The seeds are roasted and eaten, and also considered to possess medicinal properties.

EURYALE FEROX, *Salisb*

VIII

NELUMBIUM SPECIOSUM, *Willd.* (Pl. IX.)

Lotus.

Nat. Order. *Nymphæaceæ.* The Water-lily Family.

Name. The generic name is from "*Nelumbo*," the native name by which the plant is known in Ceylon. The specific name is from the Latin "*speciosus*," beautiful. The Kashmiri name is "*pamposh*."

Description. A robust, aquatic perennial, with large round leaves, and extremely beautiful large fragrant flowers of a white and rose-pink colour, the leaves and flowers standing erect above the surface of the water.

Rootstock, stout and creeping.

Leaves, 1-2′ in diam., orbicular, entire, peltate, with the centre depressed. **Petiole** erect and rigid, smooth or with a few scattered short prickles.

Flowers, 5-10″ diam., white and rose-pink, solitary and raised above the surface of the water, on long, rigid, stout peduncles.

Sepals, 4-5, caducous.

Petals, numerous, elliptic, concave, caducous.

Stamens, many, caducous. **Anthers** with a clubbed appendage.

Carpels, many, with 1-celled ovaries, sunk in the top of an obconic, spongy prolongation of part of the receptacle.

Fruit, a large, spongy, obconic body 2-4″ in diam., with a flat top, and containing cylindrical cavities open above, in which the ripened ovaries lie loosely. The ripened ovaries about $\frac{1}{4}$-$\frac{1}{2}$″ diam.

Distinguishing characters. No other species. Easily recognised by its large white and rose-pink flowers and large round peltate leaves, both the leaves and flowers standing erect above the surface of the water.

Flowering Season. The latter half of July and August.

Locality. Abundant in the Dal Lake at Srinagar.

Distribution. Throughout India, Persia, Malay Islands, China, Japan, Tropical Australia.

Uses. Almost all parts of the plant are made use of, either for food, medicinal or religious purposes. The thick shoots of the rootstock when cooked are much relished as an article of diet ; the seeds, juice of the leaf and flower stalks, powdered root, and flowers are used for medicinal purposes, and the flowers are used as offerings in Hindu Temples.

General Remarks. A peculiarity of the leaves is that they cannot be wetted. If a leaf is immersed under water and withdrawn, not a trace of water adheres to it. The leaf has a somewhat cup-like form, owing to its depressed centre, and drops of water which lodge on the surface assume a globular form and glisten in the sunshine like pearls. The leaves when picked wilt very rapidly even when their stalks are at once placed in water. The flowers open at sunrise and close at sunset, but when once fully expanded they only last for a day and then fall to pieces.

NELUMBIUM SPECIOSUM, *Willd.*

IX

PAPAVER NUDICAULE, *Linn.* (Pl. x.)

Iceland Poppy.

Nat. Order. *Papaveraceæ.* The Poppy Family.

Name. The generic name is the Latin word for "Poppy." The specific name is from the Latin "*nudus*," naked, and "*caulis*," a stem.

Description. A very graceful, slender Alpine perennial with only radical leaves, and large yellow or orange coloured flowers which are solitary on long, leafless, slender scapes.

Leaves, all radical, 2-6″ in length, obovate or oblong, pinnatifid, hairy, long petioled.

Flowers, bright-yellow or orange, 2-3″ diam., solitary on long, slender scapes. **Scapes,** 6-12″ in length, several, densely hairy with very dark-brown hairs on the upper part. **Flowerbuds,** nodding.

Sepals, 2, caducous, ovate-oblong, obtuse, densely covered with long, dark-brown or almost black hairs.

Petals, 4, large, rounded, entire, crumpled.

Stamens, many.

Carpels, united, forming a 1-celled ovary with a large persistent stigma with radiating lobes.

Fruit, an obovoid capsule $\frac{1}{2}$-$\frac{3}{4}$″ in length, covered with stiff, dark hairs, and opening by small valves below the lobes of the persistent stigma.

Distinguishing characters. Its yellow or orange flowers distinguish it easily from other species.

Flowering Season. July, August.

Locality. At elevations above 11,000′, usually on stony beds of streams, *e.g.*, Astan Marg, Zojpal, Tahjwaz, Kolohoi.

PAPAVER NUDICAULE—*continued.*

Distribution. Western Thibet, 16-17,000′ ; Afghanistan, Mountains of Central and North Europe, North Asia, Arctic regions.

PAPAVER NUDICAULE, *Linn.*

X

CORYDALIS DIPHYLLA, *Wall.* (Pl. XI.)

Purple Corydalis.

Nat. Order. *Fumariaceæ.*

Name. In Hooker's *Flora of British India* the plant is included under *C. rutæfolia* (*Sibth.*) The generic name is from the Greek "*korudalos*," a lark, referring to a supposed resemblance of the spur of the flower with the spur of the lark.

Description. A small, herbaceous plant with a deeply buried globose tuber, two opposite much-divided leaves, and a terminal raceme of red-purple spurred flowers.

Rootstock, a globose tuber.

Stem, 3-8″, erect, unbranched, stout and succulent, often mottled with red-purple.

Leaves, radical nil, cauline 2 opposite, petioled, the petiole $\frac{1}{4}$-1$\frac{1}{2}$″ in length; 2 or 3 ternately compound; the segments $\frac{1}{4}$-1″ in length, ovate, lanceolate or linear, entire, glabrous, parallel-veined.

Flowers, $\frac{3}{4}$-1″ in length, red-purple of varying shades with darker purple tips, the spur usually paler or white; in racemes of 5-12 flowers. **Pedicels,** $\frac{1}{2}$-1$\frac{1}{2}$″ in length, becoming longer in fruit, stout and erect.

Sepals, 2 minute, pale-purple, $\frac{1}{10}$″ diam., rounded with irregularly toothed margins.

Petals, 4 (2 outer and 2 inner). The two outer ones dissimilar and without wings, the lower one (anticous) orbicular, emarginate, about $\frac{1}{2}$″ in width, flat or concave: the upper one (posticous) spurred; spur straight or curved, inflated, obtuse, about equal in length to the petals; the two inner petals smaller, connivent, keeled and with filiform claws.

CORYDALIS DIPHYLLA—*continued.*

Stamens, 6, diadelphous (*i.e.*, in two bundles), the posterior bundle with a basal spur enclosed in the spur of the posticous petal.

Carpels, united. **Ovary,** 1-celled, style filiform, shorter than the ovary. **Stigmas,** 2, dilated, capitate.

Fruit, a capsule, ovate-oblong, $\frac{1}{3}$-$\frac{5}{8}''$ in length.

Distinguishing characters. The simple stem, no radical leaves, and purple flowers distinguish it from other species.

Flowering Season. April to June.

Locality. At elevations of 5–10,000′, usually on damp rich soil, often forming gregarious patches on bare soil from which the snow has just melted away. Abundant at Gulmarg, Liddarwat, Rampur and throughout the Valley.

Distribution. Western Himalaya 5–10,000′, from Kashmir to Kumaon.

CORYDALIS DIPHYLLA, *Wall.*

CORYDALIS CASHMERIANA, *Royle.*

Blue Corydalis. (Pl. XII.)

Nat. Order. *Fumariaceæ.* The Fumitory Family.

Name. The generic name is from the Greek, "*korudalos*," a lark, referring to a supposed resemblance of the spur of the flower with the spur of the lark.

Description. A small, bulbous Alpine perennial, with deeply cut leaves and very beautiful blue spurred flowers.

Rootstock, one or several small ovoid tubers.

Stems, 3-9″ in height, single or several from the same rootstock.

Leaves. Radical leaves, long petioled, usually ternately compound with the leaflets 3-partite and the segments entire or 2-lobed. **Cauline leaves,** ternately compound or partite, alternate, petioled or sub-sessile, segments $\frac{1}{2}$-1″ linear, oblong, entire or lobed.

Flowers, $\frac{3}{4}$-1″ in length, bright blue with dark blue tips and the lower portion of the lateral petals white, in short, terminal crowded racemes (or sub-umbellate) of 3-8 flowers. **Pedicels** about $\frac{1}{2}$″ in length. **Bracts** equal to or longer than the pedicels, with the lower ones 3-fid and upper ones entire.

Sepals, 2 minute or obscure.

Petals, 4 (2 outer and 2 inner). The two outer ones dissimilar, the upper or posticous petal acute, with a straight or curved spur, the two inner ones similar, clawed and keeled.

Stamens, 6, diadelphous (in 2 bundles), the posterior bundle with a basal spur enclosed within the spur of the posterior petal.

CORYDALIS CASHMERIANA—*continued.*

Carpels, united, forming a 1-celled ovary, with filiform style and 2 stigmas.

Fruit, a small linear, oblong, deflexed capsule.

Distinguishing characters. The blue flowers readily distinguish it from other species.

Flowering Season. July, August.

Locality. The Liddar Valley at 11-13,000′, *e.g.*, Kolohoi, Astan Marg, Sonsa Nag, Zojpal.

Distribution. Temperate and Sub-Alpine Himalaya, from Kashmir to Sikkim.

CORYDALIS CASHMERIANA, *Royle.*

XII

CORYDALIS GOVANIANA, *Wall.* (Pl. XIII.)

Govan's Corydalis.

Nat. Order. *Fumariaceæ.*

Name. The generic name is from the Greek "*korudalos*," a lark, referring to a supposed resemblance of the spur of the flowers to the spur of a lark. The specific name has been given in honour of Govan, a celebrated botanist.

Description. A robust, tufted perennial, with long two-pinnate radical leaves and tall erect stems bearing terminal racemes of spurred yellow flowers of about 1″ in length.

Rootstock, stout, woody, crowned with the withered remains of the old leaf-sheaths.

Stems, several, 1-2½′ in height, stout, erect, rigid, usually quite simple (sometimes with a single lateral branch from the axil of the uppermost leaf bearing a raceme of flowers).

Leaves. Radical leaves, numerous in a dense tuft of small clusters of leaves, from the centres of which arise the flowering stems ; oblong, 2-pinnate, long-petioled, almost as long as the flowering stems. **Primary pinnæ,** petioled, 2-4″ in length, few, distant (about 3-5 pairs), alternate, opposite, or sub-opposite. **Secondary pinnæ,** alternate, more or less deeply cut into about 3-6 linear-oblong or linear ob-ovate lobes, sessile or sub-sessile, bright green or glaucous. **Cauline leaves,** few (0-4), usually 2 opposite or sub-opposite leaves near the base of the stem similar to the radical leaves but smaller (rarely almost as long as the radical leaves); upper leaves small, 1-3″, usually resembling enlarged bracts, sessile or with a broad, flat, sheathing petiole, deeply divided above into linear lobes.

Flowers, yellow, ¾-1″ in length, in a terminal raceme 3-4″ in length, becoming much elongated in fruit; the raceme dense flowered and usually quite simple (sometimes a single axillary raceme); pedicels, ¼-½″, becoming longer and recurved in fruit.

Bracts, lower ones large, 1-2″ in length, cuneate, deeply cut into linear lobes, longer than the pedicels; the upper ones often entire, elliptic, obtuse.

Petals. Posticous petal, acute, hooded, with a very broad dorsal wing tapering behind and extending to where the spur commences. **Anticous petal,** more or less similar to the posticous petal, with a broad wing at the tip extending backwards to about one-third its length, concave, acute; 2 inner petals connivent at their tips, clawed. **Spur** about equal in length to petals, straight or curved, obtuse.

Fruit, an oblong capsule ½-¾″ in length.

Distinguishing characters. Flowers yellow, ¾-1″ in length, spur equal to the petals; erect, rigid, unbranched stems with terminal unbranched racemes (rarely one single lateral raceme bearing branch); tufted, radical, 2-pinnate leaves, almost as long as the flowering stems, distinguish it from other species.

Flowering Season. June to August.

Locality. At elevations of 8–12,000′, usually growing amongst boulders along the banks of streams and rivers, *e.g.*, Gulmarg, Sonamarg, Liddarwat, Kolohoi.

Distribution. Western Himalayas from Kashmir to Kumaon.

Uses. A decoction or tincture of the root is said to possess tonic properties.

CORYDALIS GOVANIANA, *Wall.*

XIII

CORYDALIS THYRSIFLORA, *Prain.*

(Pl. XIV.)

Nat. Order. *Fumariaceæ.*

Name. The generic name is from the Greek "*korudalos,*" a lark, referring to a supposed resemblance of the spur of the flowers with the spur of a lark. The specific name refers to the inflorescence which is termed a thyrsus. In Hooker's *Flora of British India* the plant is described under *C. Gortschakovii* (*Schrenk*).

Description. A robust, tufted perennial with much-divided leaves, leafy stems and terminal and axillary racemes of yellow spurred flowers.

Rootstock, stout, woody, covered with remains of old leaf-sheaths.

Stem, erect or often curved at the base, 6″-2′ in height, usually much branched and leafy throughout, striated, glabrous, usually several stems from the same rootstock.

Leaves. **Radical leaves,** several, long petioled, 6-12″ in length, shorter than the flowering stems, oblong or narrowly ovate in outline, 2-3 pinnate, usually glabrous, glaucous or not; primary pinnæ petioled, alternate or opposite; secondary or tertiary pinnæ, shortly petioled or sessile; ultimate pinnules, deeply incised into elliptic or sometimes sub-orbicular lobes. **Cauline leaves,** similar to the radical leaves but smaller and with a rather broad, flattened petiole.

Flowers, yellow, often with a few purplish veins, ¾″ in length, in rather crowded terminal and axillary racemes. The racemes 2-6″ in length and usually branched. **Bracts,** the lowermost ones ovate, leafy and incised into linear, acute lobes, the uppermost ones small, linear, entire, shorter than the pedicels. **Pedicels,** ¼-½″ in length, becoming longer and reflexed in fruit.

Petals, the posticous petal acute with a narrow or broad dorsal wing, the anticous petal acute with or without a ventral wing, reflexed ; the spur equal to the petals, obtuse, straight or curved.

Fruit, a capsule ½″ in length, elliptic or oblong with a persistent style of about half the length of the capsule. **Seeds,** black and shining.

Distinguishing characters. Its large radical leaves, branched leafy stems, axillary and terminal branched racemes, and yellow flowers of ¾″ in length, distinguish it from other species except the following :

C. Moorcroftiana, *Wall.* Branches few, bracts all large, leafy, lanceolate, entire.

C. Gortschakovii, *Schrenk.* Branches few, bracts all large, leafly, lanceolate, incised.

C. thyrsiflora, *Prain.* Branches numerous, lowest bracts large ovate, leafly, much incised, the rest all smal!, linear, entire. Flowers and fruits smaller than in the two preceding species.

Flowering Season. July, August.

Locality. At elevations above 11,000′, usually growing on the stony beds or along the banks of streams, *e.g.*, Zojpal, Astan Marg, Kolohoi, Shisha Nag.

CORYDALIS THYRSIFLORA, *Prain.*

XIV

CORYDALIS CRASSIFOLIA, *Royle*. (Pl. xv.)

Thick-leaved Corydalis.

Nat. Order. *Fumariaceæ*. The Fumitory Family.

Name. The generic name is from the Greek "*korudalos*," a lark, referring to the spur which is supposed to resemble the spur of the lark. The specific name is from the Latin "*crassus*," thick, referring to the thick, fleshy leaves.

Description. A remarkable Alpine perennial, the flowering stem bearing three very thick, pale, leathery, sessile, fan-shaped leaves, arranged in a whorl with their margins meeting or overlapping, and a short, crowded raceme of amethyst-purple, spurred flowers.

Rootstock, woody, stout.

Stem, 3-10″, reddish-purple, tapering downwards, single or several from the same rootstock.

Leaves. Radical leaves, few (1 to 3), early withering, long petioled, 2-3″ diam., very thick and leathery, glaucous (almost grey) with purple veins, divided to the petiole into 3 fan-shaped segments, the two outer smaller than the central segment, the segments 3-lobed, broadly crenate. **Cauline leaves,** 3, whorled, unequal, 3-lobed, broadly crenate, very thick and leathery, glaucous with purple veins, margins meeting or overlapping, forming a saucer surrounding the stem.

Flowers, $\frac{3}{4}$-$1\frac{1}{4}$″ in length, variegated white and amethyst-purple with darker purple veins, in a terminal crowded raceme 1-3″ in length. **Bracts,** thick, fleshy, leafy, glaucous, entire, ob-ovate-lanceolate or spathulate, longer than the pedicels.

Sepals, 2, minute, toothed, terminating in a long point.

CORYDALIS CRASSIFOLIA—*continued.*

Petals, 4 (2 outer and 2 inner). The outer dissimilar, the upper one (posticous), broad, obtuse, often emarginate with a short, narrow dorsal wing, and spurred. The lower one (anticous) rather narrower than the posticous one and with a short wing. The spur cylindrical, incurved, equal to or shorter than the posticous petal. The wings of the outer petals often shortly toothed.

Stamens, 6, diadelphous (in 2 bundles). The posticous bundle with a basal spur enclosed in the spur of the posticous petal.

Carpels, united, forming a 1-celled ovary.

Fruit, an inflated, sub-globose capsule, with a short persistent style.

Distinguishing characters. The very thick, fleshy leaves readily distinguish it from other species.

Flowering Season. July, August.

Locality. At elevations above 12,000′, *e.g.*, Astan Marg, Zogi-la, Zojpal.

Distribution. West Thibet and Thibetan Himalaya, 14–17,000′, from Kunawar to Balti.

CORYDALIS CRASSIFOLIA, *Royle.*

XV

CHORISPORA SABULOSA, *Camb.* (Pl. XVI.)

Nat. Order. *Cruciferæ.* The Wallflower Family.

Name. The generic name is from the Greek "*chorizo*," to separate, and "*sporos*," a seed, and refers to the cells of the pod each containing a single seed.

Description. A small, tufted Alpine perennial with only radical leaves and one or several leafless scapes bearing racemes of sweet-scented flowers, which are either white, yellowish or reddish-purple.

Stem, no stem except the leafless, flowering scapes.

Leaves, all radical, 2-3″ in length, tufted, oblong-lanceolate, usually pinnatifid, sometimes entire or toothed, lobes obtuse, rather thick and succulent, petiole broad.

Flowers, $\frac{3}{8}$″ diam., white, yellowish or reddish-purple, in racemes on leafless glandular-hairy scapes 3-6″ in length. Pedicels slender about $\frac{1}{2}$″.

Sepals, 4, erect, the lateral ones slightly saccate, green or purple.

Petals, 4, limb emarginate, spreading, narrowed to a slender claw.

Stamens, 6.

Ovary, superior.

Fruit, a torulose pod of $\frac{1}{2}$-$\frac{3}{4}$″ in length with a short, slender beak, the pod straight, curved or twisted.

Distinguishing characters. Leaves all radical with flowers on leafless scapes distinguish it from other species.

Flowering Season. July, August.

Locality. At elevations above 10,000′, *e.g.*, Kolohoi, Sonsa Nag and upper part of the Ferozepore Nala.

Distribution. Western Himalaya from Kashmir to Kunawar, and West Thibet, 10–17,000′; Afghanistan.

CHORISPORA SABULOSA, *Camb.*

XVI

HEDYSARUM CACHEMIRIANUM, *Benth.*

Kashmir Hedysarum. (Pl. XVII.)

Nat. Order. *Leguminoseæ.* The Pea Family.

Name. The generic name is from the Greek " *hedus*," sweet, and " *aroma*," spice.

Description. A robust, erect perennial, with pinnate leaves, and flowers of a deep rose-purple colour, in long peduncled compact racemes.

Stem, erect, 1-2′ in height, glabrous, stout.

Leaves, 6-12″ in length, alternate, odd-pinnate with 21-27 leaflets. The leaflets, thin, linear-oblong, very shortly petioled, apiculate, ¾-1¼″ in length. **Stipules,** scarious, about 1″ in length, no stipellæ at the base of the leaflets.

Flowers, 1″ in length, deep rose-purple, very shortly pedicelled, in long peduncled, axillary, densely compact racemes of 1-3″ in length (becoming longer as the fruits develop). **Bracts,** 2, setaceous (like bristles), protruding beyond the buds.

Calyx, downy, ½″ in length, with 5 narrow, acuminate teeth equal in length to the calyx-tube.

Petals, 5, free, unequal, much exserted from the calyx, the standard longer than the wings and keel.

Stamens, 10, diadelphous.

Carpels, united. **Ovary** linear and stalked. **Style** very long, filiform.

Fruit, a pod with 1-3 flattened, oblong, indehiscent joints of ½-¾″ in length. Both sutures with a distinct, entire wing.

Distinguishing characters. The rose-purple flowers of about 1″ in length, the leaves with 21-27 leaflets, the long, setaceous bracts and the calyx-teeth equal to the calyx-tube distinguish it from other species. The genus *Hedysarum* belongs to a group of genera characterised by the fruit pods being jointed. From other genera in this group the genus *Hedysarum* is distinguished by the following characters, exstipellate leaves, diadelphous stamens, ovules several, leaves imparipinnate.

Flowering Season. July, August.

Locality. At elevations of 11–13,000′, *e.g.*, Astan Marg, Zojpal.

Distribution. Not outside of Kashmir.

HEDYSARUM CACHEMIRIANUM, *Benth.*

GEUM ELATUM, *Wall.* (Pl. XVIII.)

Large Himalayan Avens.

Nat. Order. *Rosaceæ.* The Rose Family.

Name. The generic name is derived from the Greek "*geuo*," to taste, the roots being aromatic. The English name for the British species of this genus is "Avens." In Kashmir it is known as "Googemool."

Description. A handsome, robust, sub-Alpine perennial, with pinnatisect radical leaves, and large bright yellow Potentilla-like flowers.

Rootstock, stout, woody.

Stem, erect, 12-18″ in height.

Leaves. **Radical leaves,** crowded, 4-12″ in length, sparingly hairy, ob-lanceolate, pinnatisect; the segments shortly lobed and crenate or serrate, small below and gradually increasing in size from below upwards to 1″ in length, with smaller segments between the large ones, the terminal segment the largest. **Stem leaves,** few, similar to the radical leaves but smaller. **Stipules,** adnate to the petiole.

Flowers, 1-1$\frac{3}{4}$″ diam., bright yellow, few, usually about 1-6, with 5 sepal-like bracteoies.

Calyx, persistent, 5-lobed, the lobes acute, silky and spreading in fruit.

Petals, 5, free, orbicular, slightly emarginate, much exceeding the calyx.

Stamens, many.

Carpels, many, sessile on the base of the calyx, clothed with long, silky hairs. Styles become much prolonged in fruit.

Fruit, many ellipsoid achenes, acute at both ends, hairy, with straight, elongated (not hooked) styles $\frac{1}{3}$″ in length.

Distinguishing characters. The large flowers and straight (not hooked) styles easily distinguish it from *G. urbanum*, the only other species. It is frequently mistaken for a *Potentilla*, but differs from this genus by the styles becoming much elongated in the fruit. *Potentilla argyrophylla*, which has very similar large yellow flowers, has quite different leaves, namely, compound leaves with 3 leaflets.

Flowering Season. July to September.

Locality. Abundant at Gulmarg, Sonamarg, Astan Marg, Zojpal and throughout the Valley at 9–12,000′.

Distribution. Sub-Alpine and Alpine Himalaya, from Kashmir to Sikkim.

Uses. The root possesses valuable medicinal properties, being astringent, tonic and antiseptic. The dried root of *Geum urbanum* (the common Avens or Herb Bennett) has a faint odour resembling cloves and contains the substance, "*eugenol*" (which forms 90 per cent. of oil of cloves), and a glucoside, "*gein*." It is probable that the same substances are present in the root of *Geum elatum*, as its uses are the same as those of *G. urbanum*.

GEUM ELATUM, *Wall.*

XVIII

POTENTILLA NEPALENSIS, *Hook.*

Red Nepalese Potentilla. (Pl. XIX.)

Nat. Order. *Rosaceæ.* The Rose Family.

Name. The generic name is from the Latin word "*potens*," meaning powerful, referring to the medicinal properties of some species. The plant is known locally as " Rattanjot " in Punjabi.

Description. A perennial with the leaves digitately divided into 5 separate leaflets and the flowers of a beautiful crimson-red colour.

Rootstock, woody.

Stem, erect, 1-2′ in height (sometimes straggling through other plants and up to 4 or 5′ in length), leafy, branched, densely hairy to almost glabrous.

Leaves, long-petioled, digitately divided into 5 separate leaflets (sometimes only 3 on upper part of the stem). **Leaflets,** 1-3″ × $\frac{1}{4}$-1$\frac{1}{4}$″, obovate or elliptic-obovate, green on both surfaces, usually obtuse, coarsely serrate, base entire. **Stipules,** $\frac{3}{4}$-1″ ovate or oblong, adnate to the petiole, lower entire, upper lobed.

Flowers, $\frac{2}{3}$-1$\frac{1}{4}$″ diam., crimson-red, sometimes variegated with white on the lower portion of the petals, pedicelled, in dichotomous panicles of few flowers. **Bracteoles, 5,** obtuse, sepal-like immediately under the calyx.

Calyx, persistent, 5-lobed, the lobes acute, valvate in bud.

Petals, 5, free, ob-cordate, spreading, exceeding the calyx.

Stamens, many.

Carpels, many.

Fruit, of many minute, wrinkled achenes on a globose, hairy, dry receptacle. The achenes not concealed by the hairs of the receptacle.

Distinguishing characters. The red flowers and the leaves digitately divided into 5 leaflets distinguish it from other species.

Flowering Season. July, August.

Locality. Throughout the Valley at 7–9,000′, Gulmarg, Pahlgam.

Distribution. Western Temperate Himalaya from Kashmir to Kumaon.

Uses. The roots possess medicinal properties. The plant has long been cultivated in gardens and much hybridised.

POTENTILLA NEPALENSIS, *Hook.*

XIX

POTENTILLA CURVISETA, *Hook.* (Pl. xx.)

Nat. Order. *Rosaceæ.* The Rose Family.

Name. The generic name is from the Latin " *potens*," powerful, referring to the medicinal properties of some species. The specific name is from the Latin " *curvus*," bent, and " *seta*," a bristle, referring to the recurved bristles on the rootstock.

Description. A small, tufted Alpine perennial, 2-3″ in height, the leaves divided into 3 narrow leaflets with 3 acute teeth at their tips, and the flowers bright yellow and about 1″ in diameter.

Rootstock, stout, woody, branched, crowned with curved bristles, the remains of the old leaf-stalks.

Stems, many, tufted.

Leaves, 2-3″ in length, silky, divided digitately into 3 leaflets. **Leaflets,** ½-1″ × ¼″, sub-erect, linear-cuneate, tip truncate, with 3 acute teeth. **Stipules,** adnate to the petiole, forming a narrow wing on either side extending half-way up the petiole and ending in 2 short acute teeth.

Flowers, ¾-1″ diam., bright yellow on slender pedicels.

Bracteoles, 5, oblong, sepal-like.

Calyx, silky, 5-lobed, the lobes lanceolate, acuminate, much larger than the bracteoles.

Petals, 5, ob-cordate, much exceeding the calyx.

Stamens, many.

Carpels, many, hairy.

Fruit, 5-6 achenes on a flat, densely hairy receptacle. The achenes large, hairy, obliquely ovoid, not concealed by the hairs of the receptacle.

POTENTILLA CURVISETA—*continued.*

Distinguishing characters. The leaves digitately divided into 3 narrow leaflets with truncate 3-toothed tips, and the stipules forming a narrow wing extending half-way up the petiole, distinguish it from other species. It is the only Himalayan species of *Potentilla* with hairy carpels.

Flowering Season. July, August.

Locality. At elevations above 12,000′, growing in crevices of precipitous rock-cliffs ; *e.g.*, Astan Marg, Apharwat.

Distribution. Not outside of Kashmir.

POTENTILLA CURVISETA. *Hook.*

XX

SAXIFRAGA SIBIRICA, *Linn.* (Pl. xxi.)

White Siberian Saxifrage.

Nat. Order. *Saxifragaceæ.*

Name. The generic name is from the Latin " *saxum*," a stone, and " *frango*," to break, referring to a characteristic of some species of growing on rocks and splitting them by the penetration of their stout, woody rootstocks into the rock crevices. The local Punjabi name for *Saxifraga ligulata* in the Murree Hills is " pattarmar," meaning to break rocks.

Description. A slender, graceful plant, 4-10″ in height with corymbs of white flowers.

Stems, 4-10″ in height, erect, solitary or several, very slender, pubescent or glandular hairy, frequently with bulbils at the base from which new plants are developed, forming dense tufts.

Leaves. Radical leaves, ½-1½″ diam., petioled, reniform, with 5-9 acute or obtuse shallow lobes. **Cauline leaves,** few, alternate, similar to the radical leaves but smaller, the uppermost frequently narrow, without lobes, often with glandular hairs on the lower surface and margins. No bulbils in axils of the upper leaves.

Flowers, white, about ½-¾″ diam., few, usually about 1-5 (sometimes more) on long pedicels forming a corymb.

Bracts, 2, unequal at the base of the pedicels.

Calyx, adnate to the base of the ovary, 5-fid almost to the base, the lobes narrow, acute and erect in fruit, frequently glandular hairy.

Petals, 5, free, exceeding the calyx.

Stamens, 10.

Carpels, 2, united below, each narrowed upwards into a style with a lateral sub-capitate stigma.

Fruit, a capsule, the carpels opening ventrally at the top.

Distinguishing characters. The white corymbose flowers on a slender, erect stem, bearing a few alternate petioled leaves, distinguish it from other species, except *S. odontophylla, Hook, F. & T.*, to which it is closely allied.

S. sibirica, *Linn.* Radical leaves with 5-7 acute or obtuse lobes, upper stem leaves often without lobes, ovate or oblong, acute; flowers 1-10.

S. odontophylla, *Hook, F. & T.* Radical leaves crenate with 7-12 shallow lobes; lobes of stem leaves often triangular acute; flowers 3-6.

Flowering Season. July, August.

Locality. At elevations of 10-13,000′; usually in damp situations, and frequently on moist rocks in the beds of streams; *e.g.*, Killenmarg, Apharwat, Astan Marg, Zojpal, Kolohoi.

Distribution. Western Himalaya, from Kashmir to the Caucasus and to the Altai Mountains.

SAXIFRAGA SIBIRICA, *Linn.*

SAXIFRAGA IMBRICATA, *Royle*. (Pl. XXII.)

White-pitted Saxifrage.

Nat. Order. *Saxifragaceæ*. The Saxifrage Family.

Name. The generic name is from the Latin "*saxum*," a stone, and "*frango*," to break. The specific name refers to the closely overlapping character of the leaves. The English name refers to the white pits on the tips of the leaves.

Description. A small, perennial Alpine rock-plant, forming pincushion-like tufts on rocks, with small, white, solitary, sessile flowers, and minute thick, angled, flat-tipped leaves, closely packed together, giving the tufts a more or less uniform smooth surface, which in the absence of flowers might almost at first sight be mistaken for a lichen.

Rootstock, slender, branched.

Stems, numerous from the rootstock, crowded, much branched and often creeping ; main stems about 2-6″ in length and the short branches $\frac{1}{4}$-1″ in length ; densely covered with the closely imbricate dry leaves of previous years, and bearing at their tips the current year's leaves and flowers.

Leaves, very small, $\frac{1}{10}$-$\frac{1}{8}$″ in length, obovate-oblong, 3-angled, thick and succulent, apex flattened and with a white pit, glabrous or slightly glandular ciliate, in small clusters $\frac{1}{8}$-$\frac{1}{4}$″ diam. at the tips of the branches.

Flowers, white, $\frac{1}{4}$-$\frac{3}{8}$″ diam., sessile, solitary, arising from the centres of the little leaf clusters.

Sepals, 5, ovate-elliptic, obtuse, erect, persistent, glabrous or glandular ciliate, or often with few glandular hairs on outer surface, $\frac{1}{8}$″ in length.

Petals, 5, free, $\frac{3}{16}$-$\frac{1}{4}$″ in length, obovate-cuneate or almost quadrate, with slender claw, apex rounded entire or with three shallow lobes.

Stamens, 10, anthers short, oblong or almost orbicular. **Filaments,** stout.

Carpels, 2, united below, narrowed above into the style.

Fruit, a small capsule $\frac{1}{8}$″ in length, splitting open at the top between the two styles. **Seeds,** brown, shining, narrow, oblong or boat-shaped and very small, about $\frac{1}{20}$″ in length.

Distinguishing characters. The minute, closely imbricate leaves with a white pit at their tips, and small white sessile, solitary flowers, distinguish it from other species.

Flowering Season. June to the middle of July.

Locality. At elevations of 11-14,000′ on rocks, *e.g.*, Zojpal, Shisha Nag, Astan Marg.

Distribution. Alpine Himalaya from Kashmir to Sikkim.

SAXIFRAGA IMBRICATA, *Royle.*

XXII

SAXIFRAGA JACQUEMONTIANA, *Dcne.*

Jacquemont's Saxifrage. (Pl. XXIII.)

Nat. Order. *Saxifragaceæ.* The Saxifrage Family.

Name. The generic name is from the Latin "*saxum*," a stone, and "*frango*," to break. The specific name has been given in honour of the traveller and naturalist, V. Jacquemont.

Description. A beautiful, small perennial Alpine rock-plant, forming dense tufts with the leaves crowded in small rosettes at the tips of the branches, and with golden-yellow flowers which are solitary on short, leafless peduncles.

Rootstock, perennial, slender, branched.

Stems, slender, numerous, crowded and branched, about 1-3″ in length, covered with the dry brown leaves of previous years and bearing at their tips the small, green rosettes of the current year's leaves.

Leaves, obovate-oblong, obtuse, entire, rather thick and succulent, about $\frac{1}{8}$-$\frac{1}{4}$″ in length, sessile; short, thick glandular hairs on both surfaces and on the margins; arranged in small rosette-like clusters of densely whorled leaves at the top of the stems.

Flowers, golden-yellow, $\frac{1}{4}$″ in length, terminal and solitary on short, slender peduncles of about $\frac{1}{4}$-$\frac{1}{2}$″ in length, which arise from the centres of the leaf-rosettes.

Sepals, 5, widely spreading or deflexed, glandular-pubescent, oblong or elliptic, obtuse, about $\frac{1}{8}$″ in length.

Petals, 5, golden-yellow with darker spots on the upper surface, twice the length of the sepals, elliptic, entire.

Stamens, 10.

Ovary of 2 carpels, united below. **Stigma,** capitate.

SAXIFRAGA JACQUEMONTIANA—*continued.*

Fruit, ovoid, shorter than the petals, bursting at the top to about one-third way down. **Seeds,** minute, about $\frac{1}{50}$" in length, brown, ellipsoidal.

Distinguishing characters. Densely tufted, leaves densely whorled, forming small rosettes at the tips of the stems and yellow, solitary flowers are sufficient characters to recognise it from other species.

Flowering Season. August, September.

Locality. At high elevations above 13,000′, on rocks, *e.g.*, on hills above Zojpal.

Distribution. Alpine Himalaya from Kashmir to Sikkim.

SAXIFRAGA JACQUEMONTIANA, *Dcne.*

XXIII

PARROTTIA JACQUEMONTIANA, *Dcne.*

False Witch Hazel. (Pl. XXIV.)

Nat. Order. *Hamamelideæ.* The Witch Hazel Family.

Name. The generic name has been given in honour of a German Naturalist of the name of Parrot. The Kashmiri name for the plant is " Pohu." It is often erroneously called the Witch Hazel. The true Witch Hazel is *Hamamelis virginiana*, belonging to the same natural order and indigenous in the United States and Canada.

Description. A large, gregarious, deciduous, woody shrub, or small tree, 10-20′ in height, with simple rounded leaves, and small greenish-yellow flowers arranged in a compact head, subtended by four large white or pale-yellow bracts resembling petals.

Stems, 10-20′ in height, stout, attaining 1′ or more in diam., woody, branching, the twigs greyish and with stellate hairs.

Leaves, deciduous, simple, alternate, orbicular or broadly ob-ovate or oblong, 2-3″ in length, crenate, glabrous above, stellate hairs on the veins on the lower surface, shortly petioled. The leaves turn golden-yellow in the Autumn before falling. **Stipules,** deciduous, oblong, about as long as the petiole.

Flowers, minute, bisexual, greenish-yellow, about 20 crowded into a compact ovoid head of ½″ diam. **Bracts,** 4, petaloid, white or pale yellow, orbicular, 1-1½″ in length.

Calyx, campanulate, usually with short lobes, but sometimes truncate without lobes, adnate to the base of the ovary.

Petals, 0.

Stamens, about 15.

Carpels, united, with a 2-celled semi-inferior ovary with 2 styles, which become divaricate.

Fruit, a cluster of several 2-valved, woody capsules. Capsules $\frac{3}{8}''$ diam., tightly enclosed in the lower part of the calyx-tube, ovoid, grey, stellately tomentose, 2-celled, each cell with one seed.

Distinguishing characters. No other species. Easily recognised by the large petal-like bracts subtending a compact head of small yellowish-green flowers, and its hazel-like leaves.

Flowering Season. March, April.

Locality. Common throughout the Valley at 5-7,000′, often forming extensive areas of gregarious forest. It extends along the Jhelum Valley Road as far down as Uri to about 3,500′.

Distribution. Kaghan Valley of Hazara, Murree Hills, Chamba, Kunawar in the Sutlej Valley.

Uses. The stems and branches yield a hard, heavy, tough and elastic wood used for tool-handles and other purposes. It yields an excellent firewood, locally known in Srinagar as " hatab." The twigs are used for basket making.

PARROTTIA JACQUEMONTIANA, *Dcne.*

XXIV

EPILOBIUM LATIFOLIUM, *Linn.* (Pl. XXV.)

Broad-leaved Willow-herb.

Nat. Order. *Onagraceæ.* The Willow-herb Family.

Name. The generic name is from the Greek "*epi*," upon, and "*lobos*," a pod, referring to the position of the corolla which is inserted upon the long inferior, pod-like ovary. The English name for plants of this genus is Willow-herb.

Description. A beautiful Alpine perennial, about 6-12″ in height, with simple, entire leaves and large rose-purple flowers.

Rootstock, woody.

Stem, one or several from the rootstock, erect, 6-12″ in height.

Leaves, alternate, 1-3″ in length, sessile, oblong or ovate-lanceolate, obtuse or sub-acute, glabrous, glaucous, entire, or with few distant, minute teeth.

Flowers, rose-purple, 1½-2″ diam., about 5-10 flowers, solitary on long peduncles in the axils of the leaves ; buds purple ; pedicels ½-1″ in flower, slightly pubescent.

Sepals, 4, lanceolate, purple, sub-petaloid, free to base, about ¾″ in length.

Petals, 4, obovate-orbicular, more or less equal.

Stamens, 8, erect or spreading, symmetrical. **Anthers,** rusty-red. **Ovary,** inferior, linear, purple, curved. **Style,** bent to one side, glabrous. **Stigmas,** 4, spreading, purple.

Fruit, a linear capsule, 2-3″ in length, pubescent.

Distinguishing characters. The style bent to one side, large axillary flowers and short stems distinguish it from other species.

Flowering Season. August.

EPILOBIUM LATIFOLIUM—*continued.*

Locality. At elevations of 11-14,000′, *e.g.*, Sonsa Nag, Zogi-la.

Distribution. Alpine Western Himalaya, Kashmir to Kumaon, Dahuria, Altai, Arctic Asia, Europe and America.

EPILOBIUM LATIFOLIUM, *Linn.*

VIBURNUM NERVOSUM, *D.Don.* (Pl. XXVI.)

Nat. Order. *Caprifoliaceæ.* The Honeysuckle Family.

Name. The generic name is the old Latin name for the " Wayfaring tree," *Viburnum lantana* (*Linn.*)

Description. A large, spreading, deciduous shrub, the leaves of which when bruised have an unpleasant, fœtid smell; the flowers are white and pinkish and very fragrant, and are borne in compact or lax clusters, producing clusters of scarlet berry-like fruits.

Stems, many, woody, much branched, forming a spreading and straggling shrub 2-6′ in height.

Leaves, opposite, 2-5″ in length, ovate, elliptic or oblong, acuminate, sharply toothed, glabrous or slightly hairy on the veins on the lower surface, the lateral veins conspicuous and parallel, petioles about $\frac{1}{3}$-$\frac{1}{2}$″ in length.

Flowers, about $\frac{1}{2}$″ across the limb, white or tinged with rose-pink, fragrant, appearing before the leaves in compact cymose, rounded clusters of 2-3″ diam., or appearing later with the leaves in lax cymes. **Bracts,** oblong, variable in size.

Calyx, $\frac{1}{10}$″ in length, glabrous, with 5 minute teeth.

Corolla, tubular with 5 short, spreading, elliptic lobes, the corolla-tube about $\frac{1}{3}$-$\frac{1}{2}$″ in length.

Stamens, 5, 2 inserted near the mouth of the corolla-tube, and the others inserted lower down on the corolla-tube.

Fruit, a bright red, ellipsoid drupe, becoming black-purple when fully ripe, $\frac{1}{3}$-$\frac{1}{2}$″ in length, the stone slightly grooved on one side and deeply grooved on the other side, 1-seeded.

Distinguishing characters. There are three other species which may be distinguished as follows :

V. nervosum, *D. Don.* Leaves sharply toothed, corolla-tube long, $\frac{1}{3}$-$\frac{1}{2}$″ in length.

V. stellulatum, *Wall.* Leaves sharply toothed, corolla-tube very short, only $\frac{1}{20}$″ in length.

V. cotinifolium, *D. Don.* Leaves entire or crenate, tomentose beneath, calyx, 5-toothed.

V. coriaceum, *Blume.* Leaves entire or crenate, glabrous beneath, calyx without teeth.

Viburnum fœtens (*Dcne*), as pointed out by R. N. Parker in his *Forest Flora for the Punjab*, is not regarded as a different species, being included under *Viburnum nervosum.*

Flowering Season. March to June.

Locality. At elevations of 6-12,000′; abundant at Gulmarg and Pahlgam, forming an undergrowth in the woods.

Distribution. From Kashmir to Sikkim.

Uses. The fruits are edible.

VIBURNUM NERVOSUM, *Don.*

XXVI

INULA GRANDIFLORA, *Willd.* (Pl. XXVII.)

Large-flowered Inula.

Nat. Order. *Compositæ.* The Composite Family.

Name. The generic name is the old classical name used by the Romans for the European plant "Elecampine" (*Inula Helenium*, *Linn*), and is said to be a corruption of the word "Helenula," meaning little Helen, the fable being that the plant arose from the tears of the fair Helen of Troy. The Kashmiri name is "Poshkar," but this name is also applied to *I. racemosa* (*Hook*, *F.*) and *I. Royleana* (*DC.*).

Description. An erect, robust perennial, with a simple, leafy stem, bearing a large, solitary terminal yellow head of flowers.

Stem, 1-1½′ in height, erect, stout, unbranched.

Leaves, exstipulate, simple, alternate, sessile, oblong or elliptic-lanceolate, acute or obtuse, glandular-serrate, sparingly hairy.

Flowers, bright yellow, in a solitary, terminal radiate head 2-3½″ diam., receptacle naked.

Involucral bracts in many series, narrow, rather stiff, pubescent, the outermost often leaf-like.

Calyx, of whitish pappus.

Corolla. Ray flowers female, with long, narrow, 3-toothed ligules. **Disk flowers** hermaphrodite, tubular with a 5-toothed limb.

Stamens, anther bases saggitate and tailed.

Ovary, inferior. **Style,** 2-fid with linear arms.

Fruit, a small achene.

Distinguishing characters. Its simple, erect stem with a terminal, solitary yellow head of 2-3½″ diam., distinguishes it from other species except *Inula Royleana* (*DC.*).

Inula Royleana, *DC.* Heads 3-6″ diam., dark orange-yellow, ligules often curling giving the head a ragged appearance; cauline leaves few, distant, the lowermost with a winged petiole and the uppermost sessile and auricled, amplexicaul.

Inula grandiflora, *Willd.* Heads 2-3½″ diam., rather pale yellow, ligules straight; cauline leaves numerous sessile, oblong or elliptic-lanceolate.

Flowering Season. August, September.

Locality. At elevations of 9-13,000′, *e.g.*, Apharwat, Shisha Nag, Zojpal, Tannin.

Distribution. Western Himalaya, Kashmir to Kumaon, and Nepal; also westwards to the Caucasus.

Uses. The root is aromatic and used to adulterate Kuth root (*Saussurea Lappa*).

INULA GRANDIFLORA, *Willd.*

XXVII

ALLARDIA GLABRA, *Dcne.* (Pl. XXVIII.)

Smooth Allardia.

Nat. Order. *Compositæ.* The Composite Family.

Name. The generic name was given in honour of General Allard, who was instrumental in arranging Jacquemont's tour to Kashmir.

Description. A creeping, herbaceous Alpine plant, forming extensive spreading tufts with small, lobed leaves and solitary, white or pink flower-heads of 1-1½″ diameter.

Rootstock, woody and much branched, stoloniferous, forming extensive loose tufts.

Stem, the creeping stolens bear numerous short, leafy, sub-erect branches up to 1″ in length, on which the flowers are borne, or terminate in prostrate, leafy stems up to 6″ in length ; glabrous or sparsely pubescent or with small, scattered, globular glands.

Leaves, alternate, sessile, cuneate, incised to about the middle into linear, sub-acute lobes, ¼-½″ in length, rather thick and fleshy, glabrous or sparsely covered with long, cottony hairs on the upper surface ; on the short branches the leaves are densely clustered, whilst on the prostrate, elongate branches they are distant.

Flowers, in solitary, terminal, sessile or sub-sessile radiate heads of 1-1½″ diam., heads pink or variegated white and pink with yellow centre.

Receptacle, flat without bristles.

Involucre, hemispheric. **Bracts** about 20 in several series, ovate, acute, about ¼″ in length, green with scarious, black, lacerate margins.

Flowers of the ray (outer flowers), 1-seriate, neuter. **Ligules,** about 8-12, pink or white and pink, elliptic, ½″ in length, entire, obtuse, with 2 furrows on upper surface.

ALLARDIA GLABRA—*continued.*

Flowers of the disk (inner flowers), yellow, with dark purple tips, tubular with 5 short, triangular teeth, hermaphrodite, fertile, anthers not tailed at the base ; pappus copious of unequal flat, white or brownish bristles with split margins ; ovary inferior.

Fruit, 5-angled achenes, about $\frac{1}{8}''$ in length.

Distinguishing characters. Glabrous or sparsely woolly ; heads sessile or sub-sessile 1-1$\frac{1}{2}''$ diam., and leaves $\frac{1}{2}$-$\frac{3}{4}''$ in length with linear lobes, distinguish it from other species.

Flowering Season. August.

Locality. Above 12,000′, *e.g.*, Sonsa Nag, on rather dry, raised ground, near foot of the glacier.

Distribution. Eastern and Western Thibet, 15-18,000′ from Ladak eastwards to the Sikkim frontier ; Alatau Mountains.

ALLARDIA GLABRA, *Dcne.*

XXVIII

SAUSSUREA SACRA, *Edgew.* (Pl. XXIX.)

Sacred Saussurea or Yogi's King-plant.

Nat. Order. *Compositæ.*

Name. The generic name has been given in honour of two Swiss Naturalists, named De Saussure. The specific name is from the Latin " *sacrum*," meaning sacred. The local Kashmiri name is " Yogipadshah," meaning the King of plants of the Yogis, who are religious devotees.

Description. A short, stout, erect Alpine perennial, about 6″ in height and with a most remarkable appearance, the whole plant being covered with a dense, cobwebby, cylindrical mass of white cottony hairs, with just the tips of the leaves (except a few at the base) and tips of the red-purple flower heads protruding. The mass of cottony hairs forms a layer 1-1½″ in thickness round the stem.

Rootstock, stout, perennial, crowned with old leaf remains.

Stem, simple, stout, hollow, 4-6″ in height, much dilated at the top.

Leaves, numerous, sessile, linear with recurved tips, 1-4″ in length by ¼-¾″ in width, white cottony on both surfaces, sub-acute, with short, erect teeth or pinnatifid, lowermost free, all the others embedded in a dense, cobwebby mass of white cottony hairs with their recurved tips protruding.

Flower heads, in a dense, terminal, hemispheric cluster 2-3″ diam. of many small, sessile, cylindrical heads, embedded in a dense mass of white, cottony hairs, with the tips of the heads protruding and distant from each other. The heads are at first entirely concealed by the mass of cottony hairs, but protrude when the flowers are mature. Heads about $\frac{1}{4}$-$\frac{3}{8}$″ diam. by $\frac{3}{4}$″ in length, with many flowers ; receptacle with short bristles. **Involucral bracts,** few seriate, linear-lanceolate, acuminate, $\frac{3}{8}$″ in length, herbaceous, densely hairy above.

Flowers, red-purple, all tubular and similar.

Pappus, as long as the corolla, brown or white, scabrid.

Corolla, $\frac{3}{8}$″ in length, very narrow, cylindrical, with 5 linear lobes.

Style-arms, 2, purple, exserted, short, obtuse.

Fruit, achenes $\frac{1}{10}$-$\frac{1}{8}$″, angled.

Distinguishing characters. The dense mass of white cottony hairs is sufficient to recognise it from other species, except *S. gossypiphora* (*Don*), which is a taller plant 6-12″ in height, and has the flower heads concealed.

Flowering Season. September.

Locality. At high elevations above 13,000′, usually solitary on open bare, rocky ground devoid of other vegetation, close to glaciers, *e.g.*, above Zojpal towards Wardwan ; between Kolohoi and Sonamarg ; Ladakh.

Distribution. From Kashmir to Sikkim.

Uses. The root is especially esteemed and sought for by the Yogis (Holy men), and is said to possess very valuable medicinal properties. A decoction of the root in milk is said to be a cure for snake-bite, plague and all women's ailments on the upper part of the body. According to local superstition one person may not collect more than seven plants, the collection of a larger number resulting in sudden death.

SAUSSUREA SACRA, *Edgew.*

CAMPANULA CASHMIRIANA, *Royle.*

Kashmir Rock Campanula. (Pl. xxx.)

Nat. Order. *Campanulaceæ.* The Bell-flower Family.

Name. The generic name is the Latin word for a bell.

Description. A perennial rock-plant with many weak, ascending or trailing stems, simple leaves, and producing a profusion of beautiful blue bell-shaped flowers of about 1″ in length.

Stems, numerous and much branched, ascending or trailing, 6-12″ in length, slender, flexuose, densely covered with short, soft hairs, the tips of the young branches often almost white.

Leaves, alternate, elliptic, obtuse, $\frac{1}{2}$-$2\frac{1}{4}$″ in length, entire or with few distant, minute teeth, sub-sessile, pale or almost white on the lower surface, veins very prominent on lower surface, both surfaces covered with short, soft hairs, giving the leaves a rather velvety texture.

Flowers, bright blue, campanulate, 1″ in length, axillary and solitary on short, reflexed peduncles ; buds, pyramidal with ridges where the margins of the valvate calyx lobes meet.

Calyx, rotate, 5-lobed almost to the base ; lobes spreading at right angles to the erect, campanulate corolla, ovate-lanceolate, acute, $\frac{1}{4}$-$\frac{1}{2}$″ in length, with 3 prominent veins, the central one extending prominently to the base of the calyx-tube, densely covered with short, soft hairs.

Corolla, broadly campanulate, 5-lobed ; the lobes about $\frac{3}{8}$″ in length, obtuse, densely covered with short soft hairs on the outer surface, with 3 veins on each lobe extending to the base of the corolla-tube and rather prominent on the outer surface.

Stamens, 5. **Filaments** short and flat. **Anthers** long and ribbon-like. **Ovary,** turbinate with 5 ribs.

CAMPANULA CASHMIRIANA—*continued.*

Style thick, cylindric, ½″ in length, covered with soft hairs. **Stigma,** 3-lobed, lobes linear, cylindric and covered with soft hairs.

Fruit, a small capsule about ¼″ in length.

Distinguishing characters. The tufted, trailing, flexuose stems and large blue flowers distinguish it from other species,

Flowering Season. August.

Locality. At elevations of 10-12,000′, on rocks with the roots penetrating into rock crevices, *e.g.*, Liddarwat, Tannin, Zojpal, Sonsa Nag.

Distribution. West Thibet and Kashmir.

CAMPANULA CASHMIRIANA, *Royle.*

XXX

CASSIOPE FASTIGIATA, *D. Don.* (Pl. XXXI.)

Himalayan Heather.

Nat. Order. *Ericaceæ.* The Heath Family.

Name. The generic name is the name of the wife of Cepheus, King of Ethiopia, and mother of Andromeda, and placed amongst the stars after her death, one of the constellations being named after her.

Description. A small Alpine perennial, with the stems covered with minute, overlapping leaves, which lie close to the stem like scales, making it square in section, and with small, pure white, bell-shaped flowers.

Stems, slender, wiry, branching, forming dense tufts, 3-6″ in height, covered with minute, overlapping leaves, which give the leaf-covered stems a square section.

Leaves, very small, $\frac{1}{5}''$ in length, sessile, densely overlapping and lying close to the stem like scales, triangular, acute, with scarious margins.

Flowers, $\frac{1}{4}''$ in length, white, axillary on short, recurved pedicels.

Sepals, 5, free, linear or elliptic, reddish, much shorter than the corolla.

Corolla, bell-shaped, $\frac{1}{4}''$ in length, with 5 short recurved lobes.

Stamens, 10, attached to the base of the corolla.

Anthers, truncate, each cell 1-horned.

Ovary, superior, 5-celled.

Fruit, a small globose 5-valved capsule.

Distinguishing characters. No other species. Easily recognised by the stems with their small scale-like closely imbricate leaves and small white, bell-shaped flowers.

Flowering Season. August.

CASSIOPE FASTIGIATA—*continued.*

Locality. At high elevations on rocks above 11,000′, *e.g.*, Apharwat, Shisha Nag.

Distribution. Alpine Himalaya from Kashmir to Bhotan.

CASSIOPE FASTIGIATA, *D. Don.*

XXXI

RHODODENDRON LEPIDOTUM, *Wall*

Scaly Rhododendron. (Pl. XXXII.)

Nat. Order. *Ericaceæ.* The Heath Family.

Name. The generic name is derived from the Greek words " *rhodon*," a rose, and " *dendron*," a tree. The specific name is from the Greek " *lepis*," a scale, referring to the glandular scales on the pedicels and calyx.

Description. A small, perennial, Alpine, woody shrub, often growing gregariously over large areas, with simple leaves, and clusters of dull, red-purple flowers of about 1″ diameter.

Rootstock, woody.

Stems, much branched below and above, forming a woody shrub 1-3′ in height, the branchlets brown, very scabrid and glandular.

Leaves, simple, alternate, exstipulate, ob-ovate or elliptic, obtuse, or lanceolate and sub-acute, $\frac{1}{4}$-$1\frac{1}{2}''$ in length, entire, apiculate, green on both surfaces, midrib prominent, petiole very short.

Flowers, magenta-purple with rather a waxy appearance, 1-$1\frac{1}{4}''$ in diam., in fascicles of 1-3 pedicelled flowers ; the pedicels $\frac{1}{2}$-$1\frac{1}{2}''$ in length, stout, erect, red and covered with glandular scales.

Calyx, covered with glandular scales, 5-lobed, the lobes very short, elliptic, obtuse.

Corolla, gamopetalous ; tube short, globose, about $\frac{1}{6}''$ in length, limb 5-lobed, the lobes $\frac{1}{4}$-$\frac{1}{2}''$ in length, spreading, rounded, entire, covered with glandular scales on the outer surface.

Stamens, 8 (rarely 10). **Filaments** purple, hairy near the base.

Ovary, superior, 5-celled. **Style,** stout, red, reflexed.

Fruit, a 5-valved, woody capsule, with erect valves, $\frac{1}{4}$-$\frac{1}{3}$″ in length.

Distinguishing characters. The small, red-purple flowers distinguish it from other species.

Flowering Season. June, July.

Locality. At elevations of 12-14,000′, *e.g.*, near Kolohoi, in the Liddar Valley.

Distribution. From Kashmir to Bhotan.

Uses. The leaves are considered to possess stimulant properties, and the smoke from the burning leaves is said to be beneficial in some diseases.

RHODODENDRON LEPIDOTUM, *Wall.*

XXXII

RHODODENDRON ANTHOPOGON,

Bearded Rhododendron. *D. Don.* (Pl. XXXIII.)

Nat. Order. *Ericaceæ.* The Heath Family.

Name. The generic name is from the Greek "*rhodon*," a rose, and "*dendron*," a tree. The specific name is from the Greek "*anthos*," a flower, and "*pogon*," a beard, referring to the form of the stigma of the flower.

Description. A small, perennial, Alpine, woody shrub, with simple leaves which are brown on the under surface, and clusters of pale, yellowish flowers.

Rootstock, woody.

Stems, much branched below and above, forming a smal woody shrub, 1-2½′ in height.

Leaves, simple, alternate, exstipulate, entire, petioled, elliptic, sub-obtuse, glabrous above, rusty brown on the lower surface, 1-1½″ in length, petiole very short.

Flowers, pale yellowish or cream, delicate texture, about ¾″ in diam., in terminal, dense clusters of 4-12 flowers with short pedicels.

Calyx, with 5 short, obtuse lobes.

Corolla, rotate, 5-lobed, the lobes spreading, rounded, entire, about ¼″ in length, tube very short, cylindric.

Stamens, 6-8, included in corolla-tube.

Ovary, 4-5 celled. **Style,** very short with 4 to 5 stigmatic points rising above the widened truncate summit of the style.

Fruit, a small, woody, ovoid capsule.

Distinguishing characters. The terminal clusters of small yellowish flowers distinguish it from other species.

Flowering Season. June, July.

Locality. At elevations of 11-14,000′, *e.g.*, Apharwat, Zojpal, Sonsa Nag, Kolohoi.

Distribution. From Kashmir to Bhotan, Central and Northern Asia.

Uses. The leaves are considered to have stimulant properties. They are aromatic and when burnt the smoke from them is said to be beneficial for some diseases.

RHODODENDRON ANTHOPOGON, *D. Don*

XXXIII

PRIMULA INVOLUCRATA, *Wall.* (Pl. xxxiv.)

White Marsh Primula.

Nat. Order. *Primulaceæ.* The Primrose Family.

Name. The generic name is derived from the Latin "*primus*," first, referring to the early flowering of some species. The specific name refers to the bracts.

Description. A beautiful, small, Alpine perennial with radical leaves, and about 3-6 white flowers on a leafless scape.

Leaves, all radical, sub-erect, not mealy, 1-3″, ovate to orbicular, abruptly narrowed below into a long, rather slender petiole, obtuse, entire or obscurely crenulate.

Flowers, ¾″ diam., pure white or pale pink with a yellow centre, in an umbel of 3-6 pedicelled flowers on a leafless scape, which is longer than the leaves. **Bracts,** forming a 1-seriate involucre, linear with base much produced.

Calyx, tubular, 5-toothed, 5-ribbed.

Corolla, salver-shaped, corolla-tube much longer than the calyx, limb flat, 5-lobed, lobes emarginate, mouth of corolla-tube annulate (*i.e.*, with folds opposite the lobes).

Stamens, 5 included and inserted on the corolla-tube.

Ovary, globose, top rounded and thickened, 1-celled.

Fruit, a small, cylindric 5-valved capsule.

Distinguishing characters. The long scape bearing 3-6 white or pale pink flowers and the leaves with a distinct rather slender petiole (*i.e.*, not gradually narrowed below into a broad winged petiole) distinguish it from other species except *P. sibirica* (*Jacq.*), to which it is very closely allied, but this latter species is smaller, the mouth of the corolla-tube not annulate, and the corolla-lobes are narrow and deeply cleft.

Flowering Season. July, August.

Locality. At elevations of 12,000′ and above, usually on damp soil or in beds of streams, *e.g.*, Astan Marg, Shisha Nag, Zojpal.

Distribution. Alpine Himalaya from Kashmir to Sikkim and Western Thibet; Europe (not Great Britain), N. Asia, Arctic America.

PRIMULA INVOLUCRATA, *Wall.*

XXXIV

PRIMULA ELLIPTICA, *Royle.* (Pl. xxxv.)

Nat. Order. *Primulaceæ.* The Primrose Family.

Name. The generic name is from the Latin "*primus*," first, referring to the early flowering of some species.

Description. A small Alpine perennial with radical leaves and a leafless scape bearing a few violet-purple flowers.

Leaves, all radical, glabrous, not mealy, thin texture, slender midrib, nerves not prominent, closely serrated with fine, sharp teeth, elliptic-ovate, ovate-oblong or sometimes almost orbicular, with the base abruptly narrowed into the rather broad petiole ; blade ½-1″ in length and the petiole ½-1½″ in length.

Flowers, ½-¾″ diam., deep violet-purple with an orange-yellow centre, usually about 3-6 (sometimes up to 10) with short pedicels forming a loose umbel borne on a long scape two or three times the length of the leaves. **Bracts,** linear, acute with the base shortly produced, of different lengths, the longer ones equal to or slightly longer than the pedicels.

Calyx, ¼-⅓″ in length, with 5 linear acute teeth.

Corolla, salver-shaped, the corolla-tube equal to or rather longer than the calyx, mouth not annulate, the corolla-limb flat, 5-lobed, the lobes broad, rounded and 2-fid to about one-third their length.

Stamens, 5, inserted on the corolla-tube opposite to the lobes.

Ovary, superior, 1-celled, with many ovules.

Fruit, a small capsule.

Distinguishing characters. The leaves not mealy, with fine sharp serrations, slender midrib, narrowed into a rather broad petiole ; and the tall scape bearing an umbel of a few shortly pedicelled violet-purple flowers, distinguishes it from other species.

Flowering Season. July, August.

Locality. At high elevations above 12,000′ ; *e.g.*, Apharwat, Astan Marg, Shisha Nag.

Distribution. Lahoul and Western Thibet.

PRIMULA ELLIPTICA, *Royle.*

XXXV

PRIMULA NIVALIS, *Pall.*
VAR. MACROPHYLLA, *Pax.*

Snow Primula. (Pl. XXXVI.)

Nat. Order. *Primulaceæ.* The Primrose Family.

Name. The generic name is from the Latin "*primus*," first, referring to the early flowering of some species. The specific name is the Latin word for "snowy" and has reference to the habitat of the plant. In Hooker's *Flora of British India*, the plant is referred to under *P. Stuartii (Wall), var. purpurea (Hook, F.)*

Description. A magnificent Alpine perennial, with simple radical leaves up to 12″ in length and tall, stout scapes up to 18″ in length, bearing umbels of large, dark blue-purple flowers, with a darker purple centre.

Rootstock, stout, perennial.

Leaves, all radical, simple, 6-12″ in length by 1-1½″ in breadth, sub-erect, ob-lanceolate, or spathulate, obtuse, narrowed below into a broad sheathing, winged petiole, margins with shallow triangular teeth, midrib broad and very prominent on the under surface, dark green on upper surface and paler on the lower surface, glabrous except that the under surface has a very conspicuous narrow marginal border about ⅛″ in width of yellowish or white silvery meal.

Flowers, 1″ in diam., dark blue-purple or reddish-purple with a darker purple centre, in umbels of few or many pedicelled flowers, arranged in concentric circles on the top of a stout scape with a bract at the base of each pedicel. In some specimens by an elongation of the receptacle the flowers are in two superimposed whorls.

Flowering stem or scape, very stout, 9-18″ in length yellowish-mealy at the top close to the flowers.

Bracts, shorter than the pedicels, the outer ones $\frac{1}{2}$-$\frac{3}{4}$″ in length, linear-lanceolate, acute, dark brownish-purple, mealy on inner surface, the inner bracts similar but smaller.

Pedicels, 1-1$\frac{1}{2}$″ in length, stout, drooping or sub-erect, mealy.

Calyx, dark brownish-purple, 5-lobed, $\frac{1}{2}$″ in length, lobes half the length of calyx, lanceolate, acute, mealy, with prominent midribs.

Corolla, salver-shaped, tube $\frac{3}{4}$″ in length, limb 1″ in diam., deeply 5-lobed, the lobes broadly elliptic, entire, rounded at tips.

Stamens, 5, inserted on corolla-tube. In some flowers the anthers are at the mouth of the corolla-tube with the stigma lower down, and in other flowers the anthers are low down in the corolla-tube with the stigma extending above to the mouth of the corolla-tube.

Ovary, rounded or oval.

Fruit, an oblong capsule.

Distinguishing characters. Easily distinguished from other species by its height, purple flowers with a darker purple centre, and leaves with a silver border on the under surface.

Flowering Season. July.

Locality. At 13-14,000′, *e.g.*, Kolohoi and Sonsa Nag, in beds of glacial streams.

Distribution. Hindukush through Western Thibet to Kumaon.

PRIMULA NIVALIS, *Pall.*, var. MACROPHYLLA, *Pax*

XXXVI

ANDROSACE ROTUNDIFOLIA,

Hardwicke. (Pl. XXXVII.)

Round-leaved Androsace.

Nat. Order. *Primulaceæ*. The Primrose Family.

Name. The generic name is from the Greek " *andros*," a man, and " *sacos*," a shield, referring to the shape of the leaves of some species.

Description. A small, herbaceous perennial, with long petioled, round, radical leaves, and several slender leafless scapes bearing umbels of small, white or pink flowers.

Rootstock, slender.

Stem, no leaf-bearing stem, no stolons, but several leafless flowering scapes.

Leaves, all radical, ½-1½" diam., orbicular cordate, hairy or glandular hairy, margins with shallow, rounded lobes, and the lobes crenate, petioles 1-4" in length.

Flowers, white or pink, ¼-½" diam., but very variable and sometimes minute, in umbels on long, slender scapes of which there are several on the same plant.

Bracts, lanceolate or ob-ovate, entire, crenate or serrate.

Calyx, tubular, 5-lobed to the middle, the lobes ovate, acute, becoming enlarged and spreading in fruit.

Corolla, gamopetalous, rotate with a very short tube, lobes 5, spreading, entire or notched. The size of the corolla is very variable and may be larger or smaller in diameter than the calyx.

Stamens, 5 included, inserted on the corolla-tube.

Ovary, round, superior, 1-celled with many ovules.

Fruit, an ovoid, 5-valved capsule.

Distinguishing characters. The round leaves with long petioles and several scapes on the same plant, distinguish it from other species.

Flowering Season. Throughout the summer from April to August.

Locality. At 5-12,000′, abundant throughout the Valley, common at Gulmarg.

Distribution. From Kashmir to Kumaon, and in Western Thibet.

ANDROSACE ROTUNDIFOLIA, *Hardwicke*.

XXXVII

ANDROSACE MICROPHYLLA, *Hook, F.*

Small-leaved Androsace. (Pl. XXXVIII.)

Nat. Order. *Primulaceæ.* The Primrose Family.

Name. The generic name is from the Greek "*andros*," a man, and "*sacos*," a shield, referring to the shape of the leaves of some species.

Description. A very beautiful, small Alpine perennial, forming dense, low, flat, extensive tufts on rocks or stony ground, with very small, closely overlapping sessile leaves, forming little rosettes at the tips of the stems, and small white or pink flowers in short umbels. The flowers are sometimes so numerous that the leaves are entirely concealed.

Rootstock, slender, branching.

Stems, many, radiating from the rootstock, prostrate and ascending, much branched and crowded, forming dense, flat, low tufts not more than about 1″ in height above the ground, naked below or covered with the dried remains of the imbricate leaves of previous years.

Leaves, densely imbricate on the short, crowded branches, forming small rosettes ¼-½″ in diam., closely packed together, below which are the dried imbricate leaves of previous years; leaves sessile, about ⅛″ or less in length, ob-ovate, oblong or spathulate, concave, incurved with a hard spine-like hyaline tip, but sometimes obtuse or mucronate, glabrous on both surfaces, margins hard and horny (cartillaginous), and ciliate with spine-like hyaline hairs.

Flowers, ¼-⅜″ diam., white, pink or rose-coloured with a white, yellow or rose-coloured centre, in umbels of 3-6 very shortly pedicelled flowers on short solitary scapes; the scapes ¼-1″ in length, densely hairy with long white hairs and shorter glandular hairs.

Involucral bracts, oblong, obtuse, densely hairy, with incurved, glandular-hairy tips.

Calyx, 5-lobed to the middle, lobes obtuse, concave with incurved tips, densely covered with long white hairs and short glandular hairs.

Corolla, rotate, 5-lobed, annulate. **Corolla-tube** very short, cylindric, constricted at the mouth. **Corolla-lobes,** rounded, entire or emarginate.

Stamens, 5, included.

Ovary, turbinate or hemispheric, with a short, stout style.

Fruit, a small capsule.

Distinguishing characters. The solitary scapes, flowers in umbels of 3-6 flowers, leaves minute, distinguish it from other species, except *A. sempervivoides* (*Jacquem*), but this latter species is a larger plant with stolons, the leaf rosettes being sub-remote and rooted, the leaves $\frac{1}{4}$-$\frac{1}{3}$″ in length and the scapes 1-3″ in height.

In general appearance and habit *A. microphylla* (*Hook, F.*) closely resembles *A. muscoidea* (*Duby*), which also forms low, flat tufts on rocks, but this latter species has 1-flowered scapes and even smaller leaves.

Flowering Season. July, August.

Locality. At elevations of 11-13,000′ on rocks or open stony ground ; *e.g.*, Zojpal on rocks, and very abundant on dry, stony ground at the east end of Shisha Nag, where it forms extensive gregarious patches.

Distribution. Western Thibet.

ANDROSACE MICROPHYLLA, *Hook, F.*

XXXVIII

GENTIANA MOORCROFTIANA, *Wall.*

Moorcroft's Gentian. (Pl. XXXIX.)

Nat. Order. *Gentianaceæ.* The Gentian Family.

Name. The generic name has been given in honour of Gentius, a king of the Illyrians, who was supposed to have discovered the medicinal properties of Gentian root.

Description. A rather slender, much branched, herbaceous plant, with opposite entire leaves, and many very beautiful sky-blue funnel-shaped flowers of about 1-1¼″ in length.

Stem, slender, much branched, 6-12″ in length.

Leaves, opposite, entire, obtuse, glabrous, ¾-1¼″ in length by ¼-⅓″ in width, oblong or elliptic, sessile.

Flowers, rather pale sky-blue, the corolla-tube paler or almost white with blue veins ; ¾-1½″ in length and about the same in diam. across the expanded corolla-lobes ; usually in clusters of 3 flowers at the ends of the branches, but also axillary on long peduncles.

Calyx, about ½″ in length, deeply 5-lobed almost to the base, the lobes linear, obtuse.

Corolla, funnel-shaped, 5-lobed, the lobes about ½″ in length, without folds between them, spreading, elliptic, obtuse. **Corolla-tube,** ¾″ in length, narrowed below with 2 small, oblong, green glands near the base of the tube, opposite each corolla-lobe. No fimbriæ.

Stamens, 5, included. **Filaments** flattened. **Anthers** sagittate. **Ovary** superior, linear on a long stalk. **Style** very short. **Stigmas,** 2 oblong, short.

Fruit, a linear capsule about ½″ in length on a stalk of about the same length.

GENTIANA MOORCROFTIANA—*continued.*

Distinguishing characters. The flowers ¾-1½″ in length, pale sky-blue, without folds between the corolla-lobes and without fimbriæ, corolla 5-lobed, much branched with numerous flowers, distinguishes it from other species.

Flowering Season. August, September.

Locality. At elevations of 11-12,000′ ; *e.g.*, Zojpal.

Distribution. Western Himalaya, Baltistan, Lahoul.

GENTIANA MOORCROFTIANA, *Wall.*

XXXIX

GENTIANA DECUMBENS, *Linn.* (Pl. XL.)

Nat. Order. *Gentianaceæ.* The Gentian Family.

Name. The generic name has been given in honour of Gentius, a king of the Illyrians, who was supposed to have discovered the medicinal properties of Gentian root.

Description. A beautiful Alpine perennial, tufted, with numerous rather long, narrow, radical leaves, and simple erect flowering stems up to 10″ in height, bearing terminal and axillary clusters of dark blue funnel-shaped flowers of about 1″ in length.

Rootstock, stout, crowned with a mass of dark brown fibres, the remains of radical leaves of previous years.

Stems, several from the rootstock, fairly stout, erect, simple, glabrous, 2-10″ in height.

Leaves. Radical leaves, numerous, tufted, 2-8″ in length by ¼-¾″ in width, linear-oblong or spathulate, obtuse, entire, glabrous, parallel-veined, prominent midrib. **Cauline leaves,** lanceolate, or linear-lanceolate, or oblong, connate at base into a short tube, acute, entire, glabrous, 1-2″ in length.

Flowers, ¾-1¼″ in length by ½-¾″ in diam. across the spreading lobes, dark blue ; terminal and axillary with 1-2 sub-sessile flowers in the axils of the leaves, the upper ones close together, forming a sub-capitate cluster of about 3-7 flowers, the lower ones forming axillary sub-sessile or peduncled clusters.

Calyx, ⅓-½″, split down on one side to the base, spathaceous or with 5 or fewer fine teeth, of which one or two are usually longer than the others, linear and about 1/16″ in length, but the teeth are very variable and sometimes all more or less equal and either short or long.

GENTIANA DECUMBENS—*continued.*

Corolla, ¾-1¼″ in length, funnel-shaped, 5-lobed with folds between the lobes ; tube ½-⅞″ in length, without fimbriæ at the mouth ; lobes ¼-⅜″ in length, rounded, entire, spreading with recurved tips ; folds between the lobes erect, ovate, acuminate, entire, about one-third the length of the lobes.

Stamens, 5, extending to the top of the corolla-tube.

Ovary, cylindrical. **Style**, short, stout. **Stigma**, with 2 short oblong lobes.

Fruit, a shortly stalked, small capsule ½-⅝″ in length.

Distinguishing characters. Corolla 1″ or more in length, dark blue without white spots on the lobes, 5-lobed with folds between the lobes, no fimbriæ, flowers in terminal and axillary clusters, stout rootstock crowned with old leaf remains, and tufted, rather long, radical leaves, distinguish it from other species.

Flowering Season. August, September.

Locality. At elevations above 11,000′ ; *e.g.*, Shisha Nag.

Distribution. Baltistan and Western Thibet, eastwards to Lahoul ; Dahuria and Siberia.

Uses. A tincture prepared from the plant is said to have been used for medicinal purposes by Missionaries in Lahoul.

GENTIANA DECUMBENS, *Linn.*

XL

GENTIANA KURROO, *Royle.* (Pl. XLI.)

Kurroo.

Nat. Order. *Gentianaceæ.* The Gentian Family.

Name. The generic name is from Gentius, a king of Illyria, who is supposed to have discovered the medicinal value of Gentian root. The specific name is from the native name for the root of the plant " Karu," meaning bitter.

Description. A perennial with tufted, narrow, radical leaves and a flowering stem bearing 1-4 large, sky-blue, campanulate flowers with white spots on the corolla-lobes.

Rootstock, stout, perennial.

Stem, 2-12″ in length, unbranched, sub-erect or decumbent when elongated.

Leaves. **Radical leaves,** many, tufted, sessile, oblong-linear, 3-5″ in length, by $\frac{1}{3}$″ wide. **Cauline leaves,** few, opposite and connate at base into a tube, linear, acute, about 1″ in length.

Flowers, 1½-2″ in length by 1½-2″ across the expanded lobes, sky-blue with small white spots on the lower half of the corolla-lobes, solitary or 2-4 pedicelled flowers on the same stem.

Calyx, tubular, 5-lobed to the middle, lobes linear.

Corolla, tubular-campanulate, 5-lobed with folds between the lobes, the lobes ½″ or rather more in length, acute, or obtuse, spreading. The spots on the corolla-lobes if examined with a lens appear to be yellowish-green glands, which extend in lines down the corolla-tube, which is white on the inside. The outside of the corolla-lobes and corolla-tube is pale yellowish-green.

Stamens, 5 inserted on the corolla-tube, alternate with the corolla-lobes.

Ovary, linear, superior, 1-celled. **Style**, short. **Stigmas**, 2 divergent.

Fruit, a capsule about $\frac{3}{4}''$ long by $\frac{1}{5}''$ wide, splitting to the base.

Distinguishing characters. The tufted, narrow, radical leaves, sky-blue corolla with white spots on the lobes, corolla exceeding $1\frac{1}{4}''$ in length with 5 spreading lobes of $\frac{1}{2}''$ length with folds between them, distinguish it from other species.

Flowering Season. September, October.

Locality. At elevations of 6-10,000′; *e.g.*, Pahlgam.

Distribution. North-Western Himalayas, 5-11,000′

Uses. The root is used medicinally as a bitter tonic and as a substitute for the true Gentian root of the British Pharmacopœia. It appears that much of the root exported to the plains of India under the name of " Karu " root consists of roots of *Picrorhiza Kurroa* (" kaur " in Kashmir). The Gentian root of the British Pharmacopœia is the dried root and rhizome of *Gentiana lutea* (the yellow Gentian) which grows indigenously in Central Europe and has long been used as a medicine, being also used in Switzerland for the preparation of an alcoholic liquor by fermenting an infusion of the fresh root and distilling the fermented liquid. The roots of *Gentiana Kurroo* contain a bitter principle similar to that of the European species, and the dried roots also contain 20 per cent. of a yellow, transparent, brittle resin which distinguishes this root from the root of other species of Gentian.

GENTIANA KURROO, *Royle.*

XLI

GENTIANA DETONSA, *Fries.*

VAR. STRACHEYI, *C. B. Clarke.* (Pl. XLII.)

Nat. Order. *Gentianaceæ.* The Gentian Family.

Name. The generic name has been given in honour of Gentius, a king of the Illyrians, who was supposed to have discovered the medicinal properties of Gentian root. The specific name is from the Latin " *detondeo,*" to clip, referring to the short, broad-tipped corolla-lobes.

Description. An erect, slender herb with opposite leaves, and a solitary or several violet-blue funnel-shaped flowers with a long corolla-tube and short, broad spreading lobes.

Stem, erect, slender, 8-24″ in height, glabrous, simple or branched.

Leaves. Radical leaves, few, small, narrowed below into a short, broad petiole, or sub-sessile. **Cauline leaves,** distant, opposite, simple, oblong-lanceolate, 1-2″ in length by ½-¾″ in breadth, entire, obtuse, sessile, broad and rounded at the base, not connate.

Flowers, 1½-2½″ in length, the corolla-lobes dark violet-purple, the corolla-tube white with 3 blue-purple lines, extending from each corolla-lobe to the base, 1-4 flowers, solitary on long, erect, terminal and axillary peduncles.

Calyx, 1-1¼″ in length, 4-lobed to the middle, the lobes unequal, one pair ovate and obtuse, the other pair lanceolate and acute, the tube strongly 4-keeled.

Corolla, 1-2½″ in length, with 4 spreading lobes scarcely recurved, the lobes oblong, broad and lacerate at the tips, about half the length of the corolla-tube, twisted in bud, no folds between the lobes, and no fimbriæ at the mouth of the corolla-tube ; the corolla-tube narrowed below and rather constricted at the mouth; a small, globose, yellowish-green gland opposite each corolla-lobe.

Stamens, 4, alternate with the corolla-lobes.

Ovary, ovoid-lanceolate. **Style,** very short. **Stigmas,** 2, hemispheric.

Fruit, a shortly stalked capsule, $\frac{3}{4}$-1″ in length.

Distinguishing characters. The 4-lobed corolla, without folds and without fimbriæ, distinguishes it from other species.

Flowering Season. August, September.

Locality. At elevations of 10-13,000′; *e.g.*, Sonamarg, Zojpal, Shisha Nag.

Distribution. Western Thibet, Sikkim, Tungu.

GENTIANA DETONSA, *Fries*, var. STRACHEYI, *C. B. Clarke.*

ERITRICHIUM STRICTUM, *Dcne.*

(Pl. XLIII.)

Narrow-leaved Eritrichium.

Nat. Order. *Boragineæ.* The Borage Family.

Name. The generic name is from the Greek "*erion*," wool, and "*thrix*," hair, referring to the hairy stems and leaves of some species. The specific name is from the Latin "*strictus*," narrow, referring to the narrow linear leaves.

Description. A beautiful Alpine perennial, growing in tufts of many stems with narrow, silvery, silky leaves and pale blue flowers like those of the Forget-me-not.

Rootstock, stout, woody, clothed with the withered remains of the radical leaves of previous years.

Stems, many, tufted, erect, unbranched, 6-9″ in height.

Leaves. **Radical leaves,** 2-3″ in length, 3/16″ in width, obtuse, narrowed below into a long petiole. **Cauline leaves,** simple, alternate, linear, ½-1¼″ in length, silvery, silky, sessile or the lower ones narrowed to a short petiole.

Flowers, 3/8″ diam., pale blue with a yellow centre, in short, terminal, crowded racemes.

Calyx, 5-lobed.

Corolla, rotate, with 5 spreading, round lobes, and a short tube with 5 scales at the throat.

Stamens, 5, included.

Ovary, superior, 4-lobed with a short style rising from between the lobes.

Fruit, of 4 nutlets forming a pyramid about 1/10″ in height, much longer than the carpophore, and produced upwards for more than half their length above the scar.

ERITRICHIUM STRICTUM—*continued.*

Distinguishing characters. The narrow, silvery, silky leaves distinguish it from other species.

Flowering Season. July, August.

Locality. At elevations of 11-13,000′, usually on rocks ; *e.g.*, Astan Marg, Zojpal.

Distribution. Western Himalaya from Kashmir to the Sutlej River.

ERITRICHIUM STRICTUM, *Dcne.*

XLIII

HYOSCYAMUS NIGER, *Linn.* (Pl. XLIV.)

Common Henbane.

Nat. Order. *Solanaceæ.* The Nightshade Family.

Name. The generic name is the old classical name signifying in Greek " Hog's-bean."

Description. An erect, coarse, viscid herb with an unpleasant smell of mice, and with pale yellow-green flowers with purple veins and a dark purple centre.

Stem, stout, erect, branched, 1-3′ in height.

Leaves. Radical leaves, petioled, ovate-oblong, 6-8″ in length, coarsely sinuate toothed. **Cauline leaves,** alternate, sessile, ovate or oblong, sinuate or irregularly lobed, the upper ones like bracts.

Flowers, 1-1¼″ diam., pale greenish-yellow with purple reticulate veins and a dark purple centre, sub-sessile, the lower ones axillary, the upper ones forming a dense one-sided sub-scorpioid cyme, which ultimately unrolls, becoming elongated and straight.

Calyx, urceolate (urn-shaped), ¾″, softly hairy and viscid, with 5 short triangular teeth, much enlarged in fruit with a constriction in the middle and exceeding the fruit.

Corolla, funnel-shaped with 5 somewhat unequal spreading, obtuse lobes, reticulate nerved.

Stamens, 5, attached to the corolla-tube.

Ovary, superior 2-celled. **Style,** filiform.

Fruit, a 2-celled capsule of about ½″ diam., enclosed in the persistent calyx, dehiscing transversely, the upper portion separating from the lower portion like the lid of a box (pyxis).

> **Distinguishing characters.** The sessile, cauline leaves, corolla 1″ in diam. or more, with purple reticulate veins, calyx with short triangular teeth, distinguish it from other species.

Flowering Season. May to August.

Locality. At elevations of 5-9,000′, generally on waste ground adjoining habitations; *e.g.*, Srinagar, Magam, Pahlgam.

Distribution. Temperate Western Himalaya from Kashmir to Garhwal; Europe (including Great Britain), West and North Asia.

Uses. The leaves and seeds possess medicinal properties containing the poisonous alkaloid Hyoscyamine, the action of which resembles that of Belladonna. The medicinal use of the plant was well known to the Anglo-Saxons in the tenth and eleventh centuries. In Europe two varieties of the plant are known, an annual and a biennial one. Both varieties are used medicinally, but the official drug of the British Pharmacopœia consists only of the second year's leaves and flowering tops of the biennial variety, which are considered to be superior in their medicinal action to those of the annual variety and the first year's leaves of the biennial variety.

The species *Hyoscyamus muticus*, which occurs abundantly in Baluchistan, the Western Punjab and Scind, is said to contain ten times as much Hyoscyamine as *Hyoscyamus niger*.

HYOSCYAMUS NIGER, *Linn.*

XLIV

PICRORHIZA KURROA, *Benth.* (Pl. XLV.)

Bitterroot.

Nat. Order. *Scrophularineæ.* The Figwort Family.

Name. The generic name is from the Greek "*pikros*," bitter, and "*rhiza*," a root. The specific name is from "Karu," the Punjabi name of the plant, which means bitter, the same Punjabi name also being applied to *Gentiana Kurroo.* The local name in Kashmir is "Kaur."

Description. A perennial with an elongate, stout, creeping rootstock, bearing tufts of simple leaves and leafless scapes terminating in dense, short racemes of small pale bluish flowers with very long protruding stamens.

Rootstock, stout, elongate, prostrate, creeping and branching, 6-10″ in length.

Leaves, all from the rootstock in distant tufts, 2-6″ in length, spathulate, obtuse, sharply serrate, narrowed below into a broad winged and sheathing petiole, rather leathery in texture with a shiny green glabrous surface.

Flowers, pale blue-purple, in a dense terminal, spicate raceme, 2-4″ in length ; pedicels very short, about $\frac{1}{10}$″ in length ; scape 4-6″ in length.

Bracts, linear, oblong or lanceolate, acute, glandular hairy, $\frac{3}{8}$-$\frac{1}{2}$″ in length.

Sepals, 4 or 5, linear or lanceolate, $\frac{1}{4}$-$\frac{1}{2}$″ in length, glandular hairy.

Corolla, pale blue, gamopetalous, $\frac{1}{4}$-$\frac{1}{3}$″ in length with 4 or 5 equal teeth, of about the same length as the corolla-tube.

Stamens, 4, inserted on the corolla-tube, $\frac{3}{4}$-1″ in length, protruding far beyond the tip of the corolla. **Filaments,** blue. **Ovary,** superior, 2-lobed and 2-celled. **Style,** blue, filiform, $\frac{3}{4}$″ in length.

Fruit, an ovoid capsule ½″ in length.

Distinguishing characters. No other species.

Flowering Season. July, August.

Locality. At 10-13,000′; *e.g.*, Kolohoi, Zojpal, Sonsa Nag.

Distribution. Alpine Himalaya from Kashmir to Sikkim.

Uses. A valuable medicinal plant. The root and rootstock contain a bitter substance termed "*picrorhizin.*" The crude drug appears on the market in the form of short dry pieces of the root and rootstock of about 2-3″ in length. The drug is used medicinally as a stomachic tonic and as a febrifuge in cases of fever.

PICRORHIZA KURROA, *Benth.*

PEDICULARIS PECTINATA, *Wall.* (Pl. XLVI)

Nat. Order. *Scrophularineæ.* The Figwort Family.

Name. The generic name is from the Latin "*pediculus*," a louse, referring to the erroneous supposition that the infection of sheep with lice was due to plants of this genus.

Description. A robust, herbaceous, perennial plant with whorled leaves which are pinnately divided into narrow lobes, and terminal racemes or spikes of red-purple, two-lipped flowers with the upper lip produced into a long, slender, curly beak.

Stem, erect, stout, simple or branched, 6-18″ in height, glabrous or slightly pubescent.

Leaves. Radical leaves, ovate, oblong or lanceolate, long-petioled, 2-8″ in length, pinnatifid or pinnatisect; segments linear or lanceolate, serrate, crenate or pinnatifid. **Cauline leaves,** in whorls of 3 or 4, petioled 1-4″ in length, similar to the radical leaves.

Flowers, pale or dark red-purple or variegated white and rose-purple, ¾″ in length, sessile or sub-sessile, in terminal dense racemes or spikes or distant axillary whorls, the spikes often densely hairy. **Bracts,** pinnatisect, longer than the calyx, similar to the leaves.

Calyx, about ½″ in length, campanulate, with prominent veins, split on one side, 3 to 5 short, entire teeth, glabrous or hairy, often white and translucent with 10 green veins, inflated in fruit.

Corolla, about ¾″ in length, 2-lipped. **Corolla-tube,** slender, shorter or slightly exceeding the calyx; **upper lip,** erect to about ¼″, then bent forwards at right-angles, becoming narrowed into a long slender beak, which is curved downwards, then sideways and again upwards; slightly swollen at the first bend with a dark streak on either side forming a pair of symmetrical eyes ; **lower lip,** orbicular, ½-¾″ diam., 3-lobed, the middle lobe smaller than the two large outer rounded lobes, not twisted or inverted.

Stamens, 4, filaments hairy, anthers enclosed in the swollen portion of the upper lip.

Ovary, oblong, style long and filiform, enclosed in the upper lip and slightly protruding through the tip of the beak.

Fruit, a capsule ½″ in length, ovoid, acute, protruding from the persistent calyx.

Distinguishing characters. The whorled leaves, upper lip terminating in a long curly beak, flowers red-purple in elongate racemes or spikes, distinguish it from other species, except *P. pyramidata, Royle.*

P. pyramidata, *Royle.* **Upper lip,** inclined forwards and twisted from near the base, with a swelling at the first twist bearing two small white eyes with a narrow dark purple streak in the centre, only one of which is visible from the direct front, the other being turned behind, and terminating in a long slender beak, which is curved sideways and then upwards. **Lower lip,** twisted at the base and often completely inverted, bringing the lower surface uppermost.

P. pectinata, *Wall.* **Upper lip,** erect to about ¼″, then bent forwards at right-angles, with a swelling at the bend bearing on either side a dark streak forming two symmetrical eyes, and becoming gradually narrowed into a long, slender beak, which is curved downwards, then sideways and then upwards. **Lower lip,** not twisted or inverted.

Flowering Season. July, August.

Locality. At elevations of 7-13,000′ ; *e.g.*, Gulmarg, Tannin, Pahlgam, Zojpal, Sonamarg.

Distribution. From Kashmir to Sikkim ; Afghanistan.

Uses. The plant is said to possess medicinal properties.

PEDICULARIS PECTINATA, *Wall.*

XLVI

PEDICULARIS SIPHONANTHA, *Don.*

Long-tubed Lousewort. (Pl. XLVII.)

Nat. Order. *Scrophularineæ.* The Figwort Family.

Name. The generic name is from the Latin "*pediculus*," a louse, referring to an ancient erroneous belief that the presence of plants of this genus on pasture lands was the cause of lice on sheep. The English name for species of this genus is "Lousewort." The specific name is from the Greek "*siphon*," a small tube, and "*anthos*," a flower, referring to the very long, slender corolla-tube.

Description. A rather slender perennial with alternate pinnately lobed leaves, and rose-pink flowers crowded at the top of the stems, the upper lip of the corolla being produced into a long curved horn.

Rootstock, slender.

Stem, single or several from the rootstock, erect or ascending.

Leaves. **Cauline leaves,** alternate, 2-4″, petioled, linear-oblong, pinnatifid or pinnatisect, lobes short, obtuse, crenulate. **Radical leaves,** similar to the cauline leaves.

Flowers, bright rose-purple with a white eye in the centre, $\frac{3}{4}$″ in diam., axillary and in terminal, dense racemes or heads.

Bracts, leaf-like.

Calyx, tubular, $\frac{1}{3}$-$\frac{1}{2}$″ with small, crested lobes, hairy or almost glabrous.

Corolla, rose-purple with a white eye. **Corolla-tube** very slender, 3-6 times as long as the calyx, sometimes 2″ in length. **Upper lip,** glabrous, in the form of a slender annular horn, gradually narrowed from the base to the tip, not inflated in the middle; **lower lip,** 3-lobed, the two outer larger than the middle one, which is emarginate.

Stamens, 4.

Ovary, superior, 2-celled.

Fruit, a capsule, $\frac{1}{3}$-$\frac{1}{2}$″ in length.

Distinguishing characters. Alternate leaves, bright rose-purple flowers with a white eye, and corolla-tube more than twice the length of the calyx distinguishes it from other species.

Flowering Season. July, August.

Locality. At elevations of 8-13,000′, usually on damp or marshy ground; *e.g.*, Gulmarg, Sonamarg, Zojpal.

Distribution. From Kashmir to Sikkim; Afghanistan.

Uses. Said to be used for medicinal purposes.

PEDICULARIS SIPHONANTHA, *Don*.

XLVII

PEDICULARIS VERSICOLOR, *Wahlb.*

Variegated Lousewort. (Pl. XLVIII.)

Nat. Order. *Scrophularineæ.* The Figwort Family.

Name. The generic name is from the Latin "*pediculus*," a louse, referring to the ancient erroneous belief that certain plants of this genus infect sheep with lice. The English name for plants of this genus is "Lousewort." The specific name is the Latin word for variegated, referring to the colour of the corolla.

Description. A short, rather stout, Alpine perennial, with chiefly radical leaves which are narrow and deeply cut into narrow lobes, and with a terminal, dense raceme of pale yellow flowers with reddish-purple tips.

Stem, erect, simple, stout, 1-6″ in height, with few leaves, densely hairy, often reddish in colour.

Leaves. Radical leaves, petioled, linear, pinnatifid or pinnatisect, 1½-2½″ in length by ¼-⅓″ in breadth, glabrous ; lobes, oblong, obtuse, crenate ; petiole, stout, shorter than the blade, often reddish in colour. **Cauline leaves,** alternate, few, similar to radical leaves.

Flowers, 1-1½″ in length, pale lemon-yellow with the upper lip tipped with reddish-purple, erect, in a dense terminal raceme 1-2½″ in length.

Bracts, pinnatifid, often longer than the calyx.

Calyx, ⅓″ in length, densely hairy, lobes entire or toothed.

Corolla, 2-lipped, the corolla-tube twice the length of the calyx. **Upper lip,** erect, ⅓″ in length, compressed, linear-oblong, slightly incurved, longer than the lower lip, tip rounded without a beak. **Lower lip,** ⅓-½″ broad, 3-lobed, deflexed.

Stamens, 4.

Ovary, superior.

Fruit, a capsule.

Distinguishing characters. The alternate cauline leaves, variegated yellow and purple flowers with the upper lip rounded at the tip without a beak distinguishes it from other species.

Flowering Season. July, August.

Locality. At elevations of 11-13,000′ ; *e.g.*, Apharwat, Sonsa Nag, Shisha Nag.

Distribution. From Kashmir to Sikkim ; Mountains of Central Europe, Arctic Europe, Asia and America.

PEDICULARIS VERSICOLOR, *Wahlb.*

XLVIII

POLYGONUM ALPINUM, *All.* (Pl. XLIX.)

Tall Alpine Polygonum.

Nat. Order. *Polygonaceæ.* The Persicaria Family.

Name. The generic name is from the Greek "*polus*," many, and "*gonu*," the knee, referring to the knee-like nodes of the stems of many species in which the stems are swollen and bent at the nodes.

Description. A tall, handsome, shrub-like plant with rather long narrow leaves, brown scale-like tubular stipules at the nodes, and with long terminal, massive, pyramidal panicles, densely crowded with innumerable small white flowers.

Root, perennial.

Stems, 4-6′ in height, erect, robust, hollow, branching.

Leaves, simple, alternate, entire, shortly petioled, lanceolate, acuminate, with the bases acute. **Stipules,** long, tubular, sheathing, brown and thin (scarious).

Flowers, very small, $\frac{1}{8}$-$\frac{1}{6}$″ in diam., white, in long terminal branching pyramidal panicles of 1′ or more in length.

> **Perianth,** $\frac{1}{8}$-$\frac{1}{6}$″ diam., cleft nearly to the base into 5 spreading segments.
>
> **Stamens,** 8.
>
> **Ovary,** free, superior.

Fruit, a small, hard, 3-angled nut, rather longer than the perianth.

Distinguishing characters. The tall stems up to 6′ in height, rather narrow leaves with acute bases, massive pyramidal terminal panicles of small white flowers of $\frac{1}{8}$-$\frac{1}{6}$″ diam. and nutlets rather longer than the perianth, distinguish it from other species. It is frequently erroneously referred to as a *Spiræa* by visitors to Kashmir, but can easily be distinguished from a *Spiræa* by the presence of the thin brown sheathing stipules at the base of the leaves, which are not present in any species of *Spiræa*.

Flowering Season. June, July.

Locality. At elevations of 7-10,000′, usually on open, hot slopes. Abundant at Gulmarg on the open Southern slopes, Pahlgam, Liddarwat.

Distribution. From Kashmir to Kulu ; Turkestan westward to South Spain, Siberia, North America.

Uses. The plant is said to be edible and to have the taste of rhubarb.

POLYGONUM ALPINUM, *All.*

FRITILLARIA ROYLEI, *Hook.* (Pl. L.)

Royle's Fritillary.

Nat. Order. *Liliaceæ.* The Lily Family.

Name. The generic name is from the Latin "*fritillus,*" a dice-box, referring to the chequered character of the perianth in some species, which resembles a chess-board which usually accompanies the dice-box.

Description. A bulbous perennial with narrow, whorled leaves, and large nodding campanulate green or purplish-green flowers.

Rootstock, a small globose bulb about ¾" in diam. with membranous scales.

Stem, erect, stout, unbranched, 1-1½′ in height, often mottled green and reddish-brown.

Leaves, opposite or 3-6 in a whorl, 2-4" in length, linear-lanceolate, acuminate, sub-erect, 3-5 prominent parallel veins in the lower surface.

Flowers, 1½-2" in length, outside green or dull purple, inside yellowish tesselated with purple, solitary and nodding on rather stout, curved pedicels, 1-3 flowers on the same plant.

Perianth, petaloid, broadly campanulate, divided into 6 distinct, broad segments each bearing a large viscid nectary at its base.

Stamens, 6, about half the length of the perianth.

Ovary, superior, 3-celled. **Style,** thick. **Stigma,** divided into 3 short, spreading, truncate lobes.

Fruit, a 3-celled, large, oblong capsule, 1-2" in length, erect on long peduncle, the capsule 6-angled with the angles narrowly winged.

Distinguishing characters. The campanulate tesselated perianth distinguishes it from other species.

FRITILLARIA ROYLEI—*continued.*

Flowering Season. May to July.

Locality. At 8-13,000′ ; *e.g.*, Gulmarg, Killenmarg, Zojpal, Astan Marg.

Distribution. Kashmir to Kumaon ; Western Thibet.

FRITILLARIA ROYLEI, *Hook.*

L

CALENDAR SHOWING THE MONTH OF FLOWERING OF THE SPECIES ILLUSTRATED

FEBRUARY.

Anemone biflora, *DC.*

APRIL.

Androsace rotundifolia, *Hardwicke.*
Anemone Falconeri, *Thoms.*
Clematis montana, *Ham.*
Parrottia Jacquemontiana, *Dcne.*
Viburnum nervosum, *D. Don.*

MAY.

Fritillaria Roylei, *Hook.*

JUNE.

Corydalis diphylla, *Wall.*
Hyoscyamus niger, *Linn.*
Paraquilegia grandiflora, *Drum and Hutch.*
Polygonum alpinum, *All.*
Rhododendron anthopogon, *D. Don.*
Rhododendron lepidotum, *Wall.*
Saxifraga imbricata, *Royle.*

JULY.

Androsace microphylla, *Hook, F.*
Chorispora sabulosa, *Camb.*
Corydalis cashmeriana, *Royle.*
Corydalis crassifolia, *Royle.*
Corydalis Govaniana, *Wall.*
Corydalis thyrsiflora, *Prain.*
Eritrichium strictum, *Dcne.*
Geum elatum, *Wall.*
Hedysarum cachemirianum, *Benth.*
Nelumbium speciosum, *Willd.*
Papaver nudicaule, *Linn.*
Pedicularis pectinata, *Wall.*
Pedicularis siphonantha, *Don.*
Pedicularis versicolor, *Wahlb.*
Picrorhiza Kurroa, *Benth.*
Potentilla curviseta, *Hook.*
Potentilla nepalensis, *Hook.*
Primula elliptica, *Royle.*
Primula involucrata, *Wall.*
Primula nivalis, *Pall.* var. macrophylla, *Pax.*
Saxifraga sibirica, *Linn.*

AUGUST.

Allardia glabra, *Dcne.*
Campanula cashmiriana, *Royle.*
Cassiope fastigiata, *D. Don.*
Delphinium cashmerianum, *Royle.*
Delphinium ranunculifolium, *Wall.*
Epilobium latifolium, *Linn.*
Gentiana decumbens, *Linn.*
Gentiana detonsa, *Fries*, var. Stracheyi, *C. B. Clarke.*
Gentiana Moorcroftiana, *Wall.*
Inula grandiflora, *Willd.*
Saxifraga Jacquemontiana, *Dcne.*

SEPTEMBER.

Clematis graveolens, *Lindl.*
Saussurea sacra, *Edgew.*

OCTOBER.

Euryale ferox, *Salisb.*
Gentiana Kurroo, *Royle.*

LIST OF MEDICINAL PLANTS ILLUSTRATED.

Corydalis Govaniana, *Wall.*
Euryale ferox, *Salisb.*
Gentiana decumbens, *Linn.*
Gentiana Kurroo, *Royle* (Karu).
Geum elatum, *Wall.*
Hyoscyamus niger, *Linn.*
Inula grandiflora, *Willd* (Poshkar).
Nelumbium speciosum, *Willd* (Pamposh).
Pedicularis pectinata, *Wall.*
Pedicularis siphonantha, *Don.*
Picrorhiza Kurroa, *Benth* (Kaur).
Polygonum alpinum, *All.*
Potentilla nepalensis, *Hook.*
Rhododendron anthopogon, *D. Don.*
Rhododendron lepidotum, *Wall.*
Saussurea sacra, *Edgew* (Yogipadshah).
Viburnum nervosum, *D. Don.*

LIST OF SHRUBS, CLIMBERS, AQUATIC AND ROCK PLANTS ILLUSTRATED.

SHRUBS.

Parrottia Jacquemontiana, *Dcne.*
Rhododendron anthopogon, *D. Don.*
Rhododendron lepidotum, *Wall.*
Viburnum nervosum, *D. Don.*

CLIMBERS.

Clematis graveolens, *Lindl.*
Clematis montana, *Ham.*

AQUATIC PLANTS.

Euryale ferox, *Salisb.*
Nelumbium speciosum, *Willd.*

ROCK PLANTS.

Androsace microphylla, *Hook, F.*
Campanula cashmiriana, *Royle.*
Cassiope fastigiata, *D. Don.*
Eritrichium strictum, *Dcne.*
Paraquilegia grandiflora, *Drum and Hutch.*
Potentilla curviseta, *Hook.*
Saxifraga imbricata, *Royle.*
Saxifraga Jacquemontiana, *Dcne.*

CLASSIFIED INDEX BY NATURAL ORDERS OF THE PLANTS ILLUSTRATED.

GENERAL INDEX.

GENERAL INDEX—*continued.*